Just
for
GIRLS

Just for GIRLS

Understanding Your Body
and the
Changes You're Going Through

Elizabeth M. Hoekstra
and M. Beth Cutaiar

CROSSWAY BOOKS • WHEATON, ILLINOIS
A DIVISION OF GOOD NEWS PUBLISHERS

Just for Girls

Copyright © 1999 by Elizabeth M. Hoekstra and M. Beth Cutaiar

Published by Crossway Books
      a division of Good News Publishers
      1300 Crescent Street
      Wheaton, Illinois 60187

Cover Photo: International Stock

Cover design: Cindy Kiple

First printing 1999

Printed in the United States of America

The illustrations Frontal View, Side View, and The Vulva were adapted from *The Christian Woman's Guide to Personal Health Care* by Debra Evans, published by Crossway Books, 1998. Used by permission.

Scripture taken from the *Holy Bible: New International Version*®. Copyright © 1973, 1978, 1984 by International Bible Society. Used by permission of Zondervan Publishing House. All rights reserved.

The "NIV" and "New International Version" trademarks are registered in the United States Patent and Trademark Office by International Bible Society. Use of either trademark requires the permission of International Bible Society.

Library of Congress Cataloging-in-Publication Data
Hoekstra, Elizabeth M., 1962-
      Just for girls : understanding your body and the changes you're going through / Elizabeth M. Hoekstra and M. Beth Cutaiar.
            p.   cm.
      Summary: Discusses, from a Christian perspective, the physical and emotional changes that girls undergo during puberty.
      ISBN 1-58134-037-0 (pbk.)
      1. Teenage girls--Physiology--Juvenile literature. 2. Puberty--Juvenile literature. 3. Sex instruction for girls--Juvenile literature.
4. Christian life--Juvenile literature. [1. Puberty. 2. Teenage girls.
3. Sex instruction for girls. 4. Christian life.]
I. Cutaiar, M. Beth, 1954- . II. Title.
RJ144.H64   1999
612.6'61—dc21   98-40911
                                                                        CIP

12	11	10	09	08	07	06	05	04	03	02	01
15	14	13	12	11	10	9	8	7	6	5	4	3

To Geneva Beth, my gem
E. M. H.

To Becky, Jennifer, and Julie,
my precious treasures
M. B. C.

CONTENTS

ᔥ

INTRODUCTION

ᴕ

Dear Young Woman:

We are proud of you! Why? Because by reading this book, you are taking the first step toward understanding that your body is changing. Your curiosity and desire to find out more about your body and how it works tells us you are trying to be responsible with yourself and your health. And we are so pleased and excited that you have bought (or your mom or friend gave to you) a copy of *Just for Girls*. The information in this book will be life-changing as you begin to see how God created you and the special plans He has for you as a young woman.

You are more than halfway to independence on this trip into womanhood. Think of this book as a map and directions to help you get there. You may not feel ready, or maybe you even feel scared about taking this trip, but knowing what is happening in your body will help to lessen your fears. Your mom also has a book to read. She can help you with your questions.

The changes taking place in your body, even as you turn the following pages, may not be noticeable to other people—but you can feel them happening. Maybe you have started to feel a thickening in your breast area, or maybe you are wondering about when your periods will start. Perhaps you are unsure about how everything works inside your body. Maybe you just feel cranky sometimes but don't know why.

These are common concerns among young women, and we will talk openly about these feelings and questions.

We know you may feel a little shy about reading this book too. That's okay. God made you to feel shy or modest about your body. Right now, and until you feel more at ease with your new self, you need to protect your shyness. You may want to read *Just for Girls* in private. We want you to take your time looking at the pictures and reading the words until you feel you understand everything.

This is an interactive book. That means we want you to get involved with its pages, words, and pictures. You may color in the drawings, write questions in the blank spaces at the end of each chapter, or check off points that you want to remember. Underline, circle, star, and highlight whatever parts you like, want to reread, or don't understand. This book will be most helpful to you if you fill it with your feelings, thoughts, and ideas. Go wild! Get a red pen or pink highlighter and start marking! (One note—if this book is borrowed from a friend or the library, write everything on a separate sheet of paper. Still be creative though. Use different colors of ink or draw hearts or stars around those things you copy.)

Remember to write down your questions that aren't answered in this book, and talk about them with your mom or another adult woman whom you trust. We know it may be hard to talk to your mom—a little embarrassing maybe. But, remember, she was once young like you and has felt the same things you are feeling. We are sure she wants to talk openly with you about any concerns you have about your body.

Are you eager to begin your trip into womanhood? Pack your Bible, pen and paper, some laughter and excitement, and we are ready—let's go!

No One Knows but You

We'd like to introduce you to four young women from whom we will be hearing throughout this book. Each is based on a real person—a young woman similar to you! Please meet Lori, Sara, Ellen, and Betsy.

LORI'S STORY

I'm eleven, and I have a hard time making friends. I feel very shy inside, but I get the feeling that other people think I don't like them.

I feel a little left out at school during recess and lunch breaks because everyone else seems to be having a good time. Nobody understands what I'm feeling—I'm not even sure what I feel. Compared to the other girls, I'm sure I'm pretty weird, and when I see them playing together, I feel lonely.

A couple of weeks ago I just couldn't bear to go to school. I decided to run away, but too afraid to go far, I just climbed a big pine tree behind my house. I watched between the pine needles from my hiding spot as my family called for me and searched the woods. I heard my mother's plea to please come home. Eventually I got hungry enough to come down around lunchtime. (It's always easy going up. Climbing down scared me, and the rough bark hurt my hands and arms.) Mom made me lunch and then sat down to talk to me. I remember trying to stick my hands together because they were covered with pine pitch, but tears blurred my eyes, and my hands looked really out of shape.

But that is exactly how I felt—sort of blurry inside and misshapen. Being angry with myself for not fitting my hands together right reminded me of not fitting in at school.

Does any of this sound familiar to you? Maybe you have had a hard time fitting in. God made us to need other people in our lives, and it hurts when we feel alone.

Others of you may be happy with lots of friends and activities in your life. You don't have time to feel lonely or alone! Maybe you can relate more with Sara.

SARA'S STORY

My mom calls me a social butterfly. She says I'm too young at thirteen to be leading such a busy life. But I love spending time with my friends. We plan parties and outings. There isn't enough time in the day for everything I want to do.

People tell me I'm pretty. I must admit I do have great taste in clothes. All the girls want to know where I bought my clothes, how much they cost, and all that. They even ask me to help them put outfits together for them!

I think my biggest problem is that everyone wants to be my friend. It's like a dozen girls think of me as their "best friend." The other day one of my friends got mad because I went with another friend to the mall. It's not like I belong to either of them. But when they started to yell at each other, I was so embarrassed I just wanted to crawl into a hole and cover my ears. I feel as if it's all my fault, but somehow I don't want to be friends with either of them anymore.

Do you have lots of friends like Sara? Have you ever been the cause of other friends being jealous? It may make you sad and wish everyone could just get along.

Maybe you just feel sad about yourself sometimes. Perhaps you can understand how Ellen feels.

ELLEN'S STORY

First you gotta know I can't stand my name. Ellen, Ellie, Elevator, El . . . Elephant. That's the worst. Fat, slow, wrinkly, uncoordinated, and sort of gray all over.

I don't understand my body. I really don't eat a lot. I don't even really like sweets. I ride my bike and take walks with my dog, but I just seem to stay the same weight. My mom says I'm perfect just the way I am and that when I turn fourteen in two years, my "hormones will kick in," and I'll slim down. But what if I don't? What if I'm destined to stay fat all my life?

Actually I have a secret. When kids at school start calling me "Elephant," I just remind myself of my special talent. I can draw—not just pictures but anything I see. The other day a boy in my music class started calling me "Ellie." I think he looks like a clown because he has bright red hair, so in my mind I drew a picture of him with a huge, red nose, baggy pants, and floppy black shoes. He got sort of mad when I started to laugh. I couldn't help it. He looked so funny in my made-up picture. So whenever kids start bugging me, I mentally draw a picture of them looking really goofy, and then I laugh. And I always remind myself that elephants never forget!

Do you have a special talent like Ellen's that helps you feel

good about yourself? That's great! Everyone has God-given
gifts and talents.

One of Betsy's gifts is an athletic body. Here's what she
has to say.

BETSY'S STORY

*I love sports—any kind, playing or watching. It's so great to
run the hardest you ever thought you could and then score a soc-
cer goal! Or to watch a softball coming right at you, almost as
if it were in slow motion, and watch the bat in your hands
swinging out in a perfect arc and squarely hit the ball, sending
it flying past the pitcher and second-base girl. I love it!*

*My mom thinks I might be a little too competitive for a four-
teen-year-old girl, but my dad comes to most of my games and
cheers for me. My coaches always seem a little surprised at how
good I am because I'm pretty short. I remember when I started
in Little League T-ball, the coach thought I was more suited to
gymnastics because I was "so tiny." Hah! That just made me
more certain I wanted to play! And did I ever show him. Now
I'm the first pick on any team I try out for.*

*I started my period about six months ago. I've only had it a
few times, but each time it has made me feel funny about being
such a tomboy. I want to keep playing sports and playing "guy"
games, but sometimes I think that I should act more like a girl.
I don't think I'll ever like wearing dresses though!*

God has made these four girls very different from each
other. We hope that you can see yourself partly in Lori, Sara,
Ellen, or Betsy.

These four young women will travel with us on this journey into womanhood. In the next chapters we'll talk about
some feelings you may have about leaving your girlhood

behind. We'll discuss why God designed you as a woman and how you can learn to like yourself as He created you. We'll help you to have a clearer understanding of the functioning of your womanly parts—inside and out. We know that your periods are a concern for you, so we'll answer your questions about what to expect. We'll say a few words about boys and what's going on with them at this same age. We'll discuss sexual maturity and how God designed your sexual feelings to be expressed. We'll even talk about things you can do to stay safe and healthy.

By the end of this book, you will be fully equipped to become a woman of God. As a spring flower pushes its way through the soil, rises to the surface, and absorbs the life-giving sunlight and moisture, so you too are growing, stretching, deepening your roots, and blossoming into a summer beauty.

What Others Can Do for You

This book is about you—what's going on in your life, your body, your mind, and your soul. It's written for you personally—to help you with your questions, concerns, dreams, and ideas. But we would be offering you only half of the available solutions and resources if we said that all you need to navigate your entrance into womanhood are the words, pictures, and suggestions in this book.

Much more help is available to you. We know you may feel isolated or alone at times during the coming years, but you really aren't. There are people around you who care very much about what is happening in your life: namely, your parents, your church, and your youth group leaders.

ELLEN

My mom knows how sensitive I am about my body. She's always asking me how I feel or if I had a good or bad day at school. I try to be honest with her, but sometimes I can't really explain how I feel. If someone has teased me, I just feel so small inside—which seems really strange because I feel so big on the outside. I'm afraid that if I do try to explain it to Mom, I'll start to cry, and that might make me feel even smaller. But I do remember a couple of times when I

cried, and Mom just sat next to me saying nothing. She rubbed my
back or played with my hair. That felt good. It's like I didn't really
need to tell her. She just knew without my having to say anything.

YOUR PARENTS

Ellen's mom is sensitive to how Ellen is feeling. She wants
to help Ellen during those "down" times. We're sure your
mom and dad are sensitive to how you're feeling too, and,
even more, they want to know how you're feeling.

It's likely that your mom or dad bought this book for you
because he or she knows you have questions about your
body and about your life. That in and of itself shows you
how much they care about you! They want to be sure you
have good, accurate, faith-based information. This book ultimately should be a resource that helps your parents help
you. But keep in mind:

THIS BOOK IS NOT MEANT TO TAKE THE
PLACE OF OPEN, HONEST, AND FREQUENT
CONVERSATIONS WITH YOUR PARENTS!

Our hope is that after reading *Just for Girls*, you will have
questions to ask your mom or dad, or both. Trust us, they do
want to answer your questions. They've been through the
changes you are going through. Although, yes, the times
have changed dramatically since they were young teens,
they still can offer you wise guidance.

We're going to ask you to do a very unselfish thing. Ask
your parents what life was like when they were teens. Our
bet is that you'll find out some interesting stuff about your
parents that you didn't know.

To help start conversations with them, ask them what
they were like when they were younger. Did they play

sports? Did they have best friends, and why were these people best friends? What were your parents' hobbies? What were their favorite classes in school? What did they enjoy doing during vacations? What was the worst thing that happened to them during their early teens? What was the most embarrassing moment of their teen years? What was the best thing that happened to them? What kind of summer jobs did they have? What profession did they want to pursue when they were your age?

You'll find their answers very interesting, plus you'll get to know who your parents were as young adults. Most parents like to talk about their younger years. When you ask the right questions, they'll talk openly about the things that made them happy and proud and the things that made them sad. They'll tell you what they learned from mistakes and what they learned from successes.

The second reason this type of conversation is so important is that it opens the door for you to talk about what's going on in your life right now. When you've helped them to remember their younger years first, it reminds them of how exciting or difficult it could be for you right now. It gives them a more compassionate heart toward your situation.

We know, you may think that this puts a lot of responsibility on you for getting help from your parents. Some parents have a hard time bringing up certain topics. When you take the initiative, you're offering them an easy way to learn to talk to you—talk about *them* first!

WHAT IF I LIVE WITH JUST ONE PARENT?

We know that many of you live in single-parent homes. Your parent may be tired and stressed much of the time. Your single parent is doing the job of two and feels the heavy weight of this burden.

Your mom's or dad's singleness may be the very reason he or she sought out this book. Your parent wants to be sure to offer you balanced insights into the changes in your life.

Again, the way to learn to talk to your single parent is to be a good question-asker and listener first. Be sure to start conversations when your parent is able to take the time to answer. Right when Dad or Mom has come home from a twelve-hour workday is not the best time. A better time might be on a Saturday evening when you're sharing a pizza.

The hardest thing to understand when you're a preteen of a single parent is that your parent has needs too. He or she needs time alone, time to think quietly. If you want to talk, but he or she needs to rest, you can agree on a "date." Schedule a time to talk together and then stick to it!

YOUR CHURCH

The leaders in your church are a second terrific source of encouragement and support—particularly your youth director. Youth leaders have been specifically trained to understand the changes going on in your life. They, like your parents, want to see you grow into a godly young woman. Your church and church leaders can help you learn what your God-given gifts are and help you learn how to use them. They can offer you a variety of opportunities to use your talents in ways that will help others and make you feel good about yourself.

Church youth directors know how to make so many things fun. They help to take the ordinariness out of everyday circumstances and show you how to look at these from an exciting perspective. Through Bible-based instruction, they can teach you how to apply Jesus' principles to your life now.

Are you familiar with the initials "WWJD"? Do you know what those initials stand for? They mean, "What Would Jesus Do?" There are WWJD bracelets, necklaces, key chains, coffee mugs, pins, etc. They remind people to ask, "What would Jesus do?" when faced with a sticky situation. In a nutshell that's what your church youth leader can do for you. He or she can teach you to live a godly life under the guidance of Jesus and answer "WWJD?"

Getting involved with your church youth group may also provide like-minded friends. The other young men and women in the group want the same kind of friendships and support you need. They too want to grow in their Christian faith and relationship with Jesus. Like-minded friends can become one of your best avenues of support and care when you are feeling confused, left out, or inadequate. They also will get really excited with you and congratulate you when something rewarding or exciting has happened in your life. It feels so good to share great news with good friends. They are like your private cheering squad!!

WHAT IF MY CHURCH DOESN'T HAVE A YOUTH PROGRAM?

There's no reason why you can't start one. Give thought to starting a Christian club at school if your church doesn't offer a youth ministry. How? First ask an older teen or adult in your church to help you organize a club. This person should be someone who believes in what you want to do, will offer guidance and support, and will come to at least the first several meetings. Then you'll need to approach your school principal with the idea. Technically he or she cannot refuse, and most schools are happy to have a Christian club meet within the school because Christian clubs don't cause problems like some other clubs. Then make up simple posters to put around the school building—with the time, date, and meeting place.

We know, your first thought at this suggestion is, *What if no one shows up?* That is a possibility. But if you are faithful in continuing to put the word out, have an adult helping you organize it, and pray specifically for other participants, God will honor your efforts. Remember other young people your age are looking for friends and groups to join too.

What do you hope to gain from this? Again, like-minded friends who will care for and about each other and you. Nothing will relieve occasional feelings of loneliness better than the presence of another person who is feeling some of the same things you are. And when you're feeling really happy, your joy will be contagious.

Do you know what the trick is to making friends?

BE A FRIEND!!

That's right—just be friendly. How? Treat others with respect, learn to listen to what they have to say, show interest in what interests them. Never criticize, put down, or tease. When you treat others as you'd like to be treated, guess what happens? They do treat you as you want to be treated!

Do you know one of the best ways to get out of an occasional "I'm feeling sad" or I'm feeling blue" slump? Put your feelings aside, even just for five minutes, and reach out to someone else. Perhaps there's someone at youth group who always sits alone, or there's a heavy person at lunch at school who always eats alone. If you can courageously sit with that person, even for a few minutes, you've helped two people—yourself and the person you reached out to. You'll feel proud of yourself, and you'll give the other person a ray of hope. Try it—it works! And you know what else? You'll have done what Jesus would do!

Throughout this book we'll remind you to seek guidance and answers from your mom, dad, or youth leader. They want to hear your questions. Write down your questions or thoughts right away as you're reading, and then ask for answers right away. Remember: No question is too stupid to ask, and no answer is too hard to explain.

3

Puberty and You

Isn't it great being a young woman? We bet that you really like your life most of the time. Oh, we know, there are times you could just *strangle* your brother or lock yourself in your room *forever* because you need to be alone. Those are normal feelings for every young woman. But, for the most part, life is going great at the age you are now. As you read this book, you'll learn how to keep those good and excited feelings more of the time!

The four young women we met in chapter 1 are in different stages on their trip into womanhood. They each feel very differently about the changes going on in their lives. Lori is shy; Sara is busy making plans; Ellen feels blah about her body; and Betsy loves how her body performs. Just as their feelings about themselves are unique to themselves, so are the changes going on inside their bodies. Ellen already wears a bra but hasn't started her periods. Betsy gets her periods, but she hardly needs to wear a bra. Sara has started to grow a few hairs on her private area and wears deodorant. Lori still has all the marks of a young girl with little breast tissue development. What is important to understand is that each will develop fully—in her body's preprogrammed timing.

These physical changes are called *puberty*. This term is used for all the physical and emotional changes that take place starting around the age of eight and lasting until about age sixteen. We know, you're thinking, *Eight years to grow my breasts and start my period!* But don't worry! The time frame of eight to sixteen years old simply means that around age eight your body started gearing up for the changes, and by the time you're sixteen, the changes are mostly done. You won't even notice some of them, or others take so long that it's only when you think back to how you looked before that you notice the differences.

Look at these specific changes that happen during puberty. How many signs of puberty do you have?

☐ *Your feet are growing—fast. Maybe you've changed shoe size two times in the last year.*

☐ *You've begun to notice an unpleasant odor when you sweat, particularly from under your arms.*

☐ *Your breasts have changed. They are bigger or fuller. Maybe they're a little sore, or you've noticed that your nipples have become bigger or darker.*

☐ *The hairs on your arms and legs have grown thicker and darker.*

☐ *Curly or straight hair has started to grow on your vulva (This is the correct term for your private parts. We'll talk more about this soon) and under your arms.*

☐ *Your body seems more "greasy," particularly your face and hair, and you've found that you like to shower more often.*

☐ *You've noticed that your underwear seems dirtier with yellow discharge that you know isn't urine (pee).*

☐ *You've had your period (menstruating) once or a number of times.*

☐ *Your whole body seems bigger, taller, and fuller. (Perhaps your mom and dad have commented about how frequently they have to buy new clothes for you!)*

No wonder it takes years for all of this to happen! It's a good thing God didn't design young women's bodies to make the changes in just a few days or weeks. Instead He has given you lots of time to adjust to the changes so they won't seem so scary or overwhelming. When the changes of puberty are complete, you are considered sexually mature. This means that your body would be ready to have a baby if you were to have sexual intercourse. (We'll discuss sexual intercourse more in chapter 12.)

These changes can make you feel scared, excited, and embarrassed—all at the same time. We understand those feelings—as do your mom and dad. We know they care deeply about what is going on in your life. They want to stay involved with you as you grow. They want to hear about what you like, don't like, think, want, and need. They may have a difficult time talking to you sometimes if you're feeling grouchy (or if they are!), but it's so very important to keep them up to date with what's happening.

Equally important, the Lord wants to stay involved in your life. He doesn't want you to face theses changes alone without His guidance. He designed you. He knows that these changes in your life are just that—life-changing! Part of the purpose of the bodily changes is to help you depend on God and develop faith in Him. When it seems that your period will never start, or when you've had a fight with a friend, or when you're attracted to a boy, or when you're just feeling confused about *everything*—there is a truth you can hold on to with all of your strength:

GOD IS WITH YOU!!

This very second, as you read these words, God is present right beside you. We are positive of this. Can we ask you something? Have you invited Jesus Christ into your heart to be the Lord of your life?

Let us explain. We don't want to assume that you know Jesus as your Savior. If you do, great! Keep reading this though! If you don't, the simple truth is that Jesus Christ died on a cross for each person on the face of the earth. He died to take away the sins or the wrongs that you have done in your life (like having a bad attitude, lying, talking about other people behind their backs, cheating, stealing, talking back to your parents—you know what we mean). Where does He take the sins? The Bible says He puts them behind Him where He can't see them anymore. Why would He do that? Because He loves you so much He doesn't want to see you suffer from the consequences of a lifetime of sins. Instead He wants you to live with Him forever in heaven after you leave the earth.

But what about now—while you're on earth? When you accept Jesus to be the King of your life, He becomes "an ever-present help in trouble" (Psalm 46:1). Isn't it great to know that you are not alone in all of the changes you are going through? He is always with you. Every minute of every day. If you've never asked Jesus to be in charge of your life, you can do so right now. Pray this prayer in your heart or out loud:

"Lord, Jesus, I know that sometimes I do and say things I shouldn't. I know that makes me a sinner. I am sorry for the times I have sinned. Please take those sins away and put them behind You so neither of us has to see them again. I want You to now take control of my life so that You will be with me always to help me, especially now with all the stuff happening in my body. I know I can count on You. Thank You. I love You. Amen."

Did you just pray that prayer for the first time in your

life? If you did, turn to the back of this book to Appendix A for an address to which you can write for more information about having Jesus in your life.

Having a personal relationship with the Lord Jesus will make the passage into womanhood easier, because He will be with you and help you when you're having a hard time or when you're faced with difficult choices. He is indeed an ever-present help.

Go look in the mirror. Do you look any different than you did ten minutes ago? Probably not—unless you've been crying (which many people do when they ask Jesus into their lives). But you are different, not only because you may have just asked Jesus into your life, but also because every second your body is changing and taking you closer to womanhood. When you're done passing through puberty, you will look like a different person, but you'll still be you on the inside. It's likely that if you don't like broccoli now, you still won't like it when you're sixteen. But other likes, dislikes, or ideas you have now may change by the time you are physically mature.

What's important to know is that the person God created you to be is always inside of you growing stronger every day. God has a purpose that only you can carry out. Amazing, isn't it that God already knows how your life is going to work out? Isn't it worth putting your faith and trust in Him to make sure His perfect plans happen to you? You bet it is!

If you don't read the Bible regularly, we'd like to encourage you to do that. The last three books in the book list at the end of this book are devotional Bibles for young people. They have short readings of Bible passages and a story or comments to explain what the verses mean. When you make a new friend or are keeping track of an old friend, you spend a lot of time talking together, right? So it is with your relationship with the Lord. You need to and will want to talk with Him every day, and even more, He *wants* to talk to you. You can talk to him just like to a friend (He is your friend). Prayer doesn't have to be a serious time. Write Him a letter, or pray in your mind as you ride your bike. It doesn't matter *how* you do it so much as *that* you do it.

As we talk about how you can grow into the woman God wants you to be, we're going to start with how you may be feeling. As you read through the next pages, check off the feelings that you have (unless of course this is a library or friend's book—then just write on a separate sheet of paper) and jot down other things you may be feeling too.

4

It's a Whole New World

LORI

෴

I have sort of an embarrassing confession to make. Once in a while I like to play with my old Barbies. I know, it's kinda babyish at eleven, but sometimes I like to hide up in the attic where my mom put all the Barbies and just play with them, dress them up for parties, set up a house for them. You know, like I used to when I was nine. I'd be so embarrassed if someone found out though. I feel sort of sad, like I've betrayed my old friends, my Barbies. I don't mean to be ashamed of them, but at the same time I feel too old to be playing with them.

Have you had the same thoughts—feeling sad about not playing with certain toys anymore or about changing what you like to do or think? Lori and the other three girls have such feelings too—about themselves, boys, God, church, their families, their friends, what they believe. We certainly can't and don't want to tell you how you should or shouldn't feel. If you feel a certain way, then it's a real feeling, because you're an individual with unique ideas and thoughts like no one else's! But let's take a look at some feel-

ings many young women have, and we'll try to explain why
you have them.

OVERWHELMED

So many changes will happen in your life and to your body
over the next couple of years. You'll soon be starting middle
school, or have just entered, possibly in a whole new town
or school district. You know your periods will be starting
within a few years (or maybe they have already started), and
you're unsure what to expect. Your parents may be asking
you to do more of the house chores, and maybe your sports
coach is demanding more of your time.

Many people are expecting more of you because you're
getting older. You may feel like an out-of-balance washing
machine that's trying to spin fast but is so overloaded all
you can do is stop and yell the alarm—"Too much!"

FRUSTRATED

You think that you can't keep up with these new demands,
and you may wonder, *What's the point of even trying?* Sort of
like fighting with a stuck coat zipper, the harder you try to
undo the snag, the worse it gets, and the angrier you get.
Sometimes you may feel like just giving up and leaving all
your responsibilities undone.

SCARED

The years between ten and fourteen are scary because you
know changes are coming, and you don't know what to
expect. You may think that you have to make some serious
decisions now, but you are afraid of making the wrong
choices. You may also worry that with the added responsibilities, you might not do as well as you had hoped. You are
afraid of failing. Like a high-flying kite suddenly finding

itself without a breeze, you may feel as if the hard ground is rushing up to meet you.

LONELY

As Lori said, you may feel left out and alone. It is unusual for young women to talk about their feelings to one another, so you may not realize that your friends may be feeling the same way as you.

Loneliness is missing the presence of someone else in your life. You feel like a half-empty glass of water; you "thirst" for an understanding friend.

SELF-CONSCIOUS

As your body begins to change, you may be very shy and modest. Like Ellen, many girls add a layer of fat a year or so before their periods start. This is your body's way of ensuring that your bones and muscles have enough food to grow on during the changes. These body changes prove you're becoming a woman, but you may not want anyone else to notice them. Maybe you are hiding under oversized sweatshirts or sweaters or are wearing men's clothes. You might be able to understand how a turtle feels. It likes to stay hidden and protected inside its shell.

A SENSE OF LOSS

As you go through the transition from girlhood to womanhood, you may feel as if you are leaving something behind. And you are in a way. You are no longer interested in certain toys, ideas, clothes, or activities. In the past these things were a part of who you were. But now as you enter adolescence, new things are becoming more interesting to you. Likely, these new things are more mature ideas and activities. But there may still be times when you miss the easiness of your younger days. Like Lori sneaking up to the attic to play with Barbies, maybe you too play in private times old make-believe games.

HAPPY

There are surely times you have real excitement and happiness about your life or an event. Like Sara who loves an active life, maybe you too have joy bubbling up and feel sort of giggly inside. Maybe you jump around the house because you just can't keep the happiness inside, and, like a hot-air balloon, you feel you could just fly!

WEIRD

As Lori said earlier, she thinks she is strange compared to the other girls in her class. She worries that her clothes aren't right or her hair is sticking out and looks funny.

Maybe you think that you don't quite measure up either. Like a square block in a round hole, you just don't fit, and you can't seem to keep up with what is "in" with your classmates.

CONFUSED

Maybe all the above feelings are just jumbled together into a confusing mess—like a knotted string of Christmas lights. You can't seem to find the beginning or end of any feeling, and it just leads to more confusion when you try to untangle everything!

GUILTY

When you have guilt, you are sorry about something that has happened. Sometimes you may feel guilty about something that really isn't your fault or had nothing to do with you. As Sara said, when her friends fight over her, she feels sad and sort of tired inside. Like a pile of snow in the sun, guilt will make you feel as if you are melting into a very small person.

You can probably add other feelings and thoughts to this list. We don't believe we have thought of everything, and, as we said before, you are unique. Whatever you feel isn't good or bad. Because God designed you as an emotional being, your feelings spring from who you are as He made you!

On the lines below write down some of your own feelings—either the ones we've listed or others unique to you. Write down every emotion you can remember that you have felt in the last few days or weeks.

Dear Diary

_____

_____

_____

_____

_____

_____

You may already write regularly in a diary. If you do, you know how it helps you sort through different emotions as well as keep track of what you do every day.

Writing out your life in a diary, or "journaling" as some people call it, gives you a written record of everything that's important to you during this time of your life. It helps you to understand the "cause and effect" of circumstances around you. For example, if a friend made fun of your hair at school today, and you write about it in your diary and add that her comments hurt your feelings, you will begin to see the connection between situations or conversations and your feelings. Or if a boy you think is kind of cute sat next to you on the bus, writing down how you felt (happy, scared, self-conscious) helps you to sort out confusing emotions.

Try writing down one situation or "happening" at a time, and then match your feelings to each one. You will find, over time, that how you feel about certain circumstances will be very clear to you and will eventually help you to react to circumstances in a more positive way. In short, journaling will give you more control over how you feel and act!

It may seem strange to be writing about yourself to no one. It might help to name your diary or pretend you are writing to a real person. You could write to God and tell Him everything (remember, He knows all that is in your mind anyway). Or you could make up the perfect listening person in your mind and give him or her a name. It's just easier to write to a "real" person than to a blank page.

Naturally, you probably feel concerned about someone else reading your diary. Your brothers and sisters may try to sneak a peek, and though most parents can be trusted not to read your private words, you may feel more comfortable hiding your diary. We highly recommend you keep your private journal in a safe spot. But let us caution you—the first place anyone is going to look for your diary is between your mattress and box springs! Think of an unusual place to keep it—somewhere that will be the last place a person would look.

BETSY

I've been writing to myself for four years—since I turned ten. At first I wrote letters to myself. I didn't write every day, but I wrote about once every month or so. I wrote about any special things that had happened in my life. Then I put the written thoughts in an envelope, sealed it, dated the outside, and hid it in my old boots in my closet. I made myself wait an entire year before opening it. My letters always showed me how much I had grown up over the last year and how things that I had felt hurt about or had questioned seemed less important a year later. Sometimes I wouldn't even remember the events I had written about! My letters have shown me how well and how quickly I am growing up.

Whatever form you decide to use to write about your life is good. Promise yourself to write daily, weekly, or monthly. As writing becomes a habit, you will find you miss it when you don't do it. And the practice of writing things now will carry over to your adult years when it will be just as important to write down your feelings and life's happenings.

If you prefer to draw pictures rather than write about what's happening, you could buy a sketchbook in which to draw your illustrations.

Speaking of life's happenings, listen next to this young woman's story . . .

5

A Special Design

Imagine waking from a deep sleep. You are well rested and full of energy but perhaps a little perplexed. You pass your hand over your mouth as you yawn and then stretch your body. It feels good to move your muscles. You open your eyes to look around you. You are awestruck by the scene. Beautiful trees of the richest greens form a canopy over your head; birds with the highest, sweetest voices sing around you; the soft, mossy earth on which you are lying has a springlike fragrance; and a faint salty taste is on your lips.

But where are you? You have no memory of this place, no memory of being here before. Actually, you have no memory of anything whatsoever. You have no history, yet you feel at total peace inside; you know you are supposed to be here. Suddenly a gentle voice is at your ear, "Eve?"

You are silent. The kind voice persists. "Eve, get up. You are to be my helpmate. My name is Adam . . ."

Isn't it amazing how God created Adam and Eve? Imagine waking up as a young woman without anyone to instruct you about *how to be a woman?* Yet Eve knew from the start she was created as Adam's helpmate. Her role was probably clearly defined then—help collect food, prepare it, enjoy eating meals with Adam, tend the Garden, care for the animals, bear children, and enjoy marriage as God intended it. Though the role of a woman has become more complicated now, we are designed no less perfectly than Eve. We still have all the right brain and body power to do the job the Lord has designed for us as individuals.

You are purposely designed by God as first a girl and now as a young woman. This was not an accident. Indeed, being a woman is the *best plan* God has for you. When He knew you were to be created, He knew you would be a girl.

Grab your Bible and look at Psalm 139:13-16: "For you created my inmost being; you knit me together in my mother's womb. I praise you because I am fearfully and wonderfully made; your works are wonderful, I know that full well. My frame was not hidden from you when I was made in the secret place. When I was woven together in the depths of the earth, your eyes saw my unformed body. All the days ordained for me were written in your book before one of them came to be."

Yes, you are fearfully made. But does that mean you need to be afraid of your body? Absolutely not! Don't forget the word *wonderfully* too. Fearfully and wonderfully. Respectfully and amazingly. Beautifully and remarkably. Shyly and awesomely. It's as if God kept your forming body in hiding for nine months so He could perfect you exactly as He wanted you to be. With your father's nose, your mother's laugh, your grandmother's ear for music, or your grandfather's athletic skill. Simply put, you are the perfect combination God made from the people in your life (even, and especially, if you are adopted. Twice God decided what personal combinations would best make you become you—first from your biological parents and second from your adoptive mother and father).

SARA

↩

It's easy for me to recognize myself as a person created by God with combinations of traits from my family. I look like my mom. Hands down, I'm just a smaller her. But it's really my dad's personality that makes me so social. He loves parties, loves to laugh, and has tons of friends. I love to be with him when he is in one of "his moods," as Mom calls it. He makes me giggle, and I can't stop. That's when I am so glad to be a part of my family.

Look at Psalm 139:14 again. "I praise you . . ." Yes, we are to praise God for the way He created us. It's easy when we feel happy and good about ourselves, but much harder when we don't. Even if we feel too short, too fat, too grumpy, not smart enough, and so on, despite what we feel are our shortcomings, we are supposed to praise Him. But it's not always easy.

Do you know why God wants us to praise Him for the way we are created? Because we are created *like Him*, and He has so many personal features He has yet to run out of combinations!

Look at Genesis 1:27. "So God created man in his own image, in the image of God he created him; male and female he created them." Just to be sure we don't miss this truth, the verse states it twice. God created man and woman to be like Him—to think, to have emotions, to have gifts and talents, to be creative, to love.

Imagine God standing before a huge canvas. He has a painting palette in one hand and a giant paintbrush in the other. As He prepares to paint a picture, He mixes a few colors together on His palette to create a new hue He's never used before. He tilts His head, deciding if it's just right. Yes, it is. With broad, firm strokes He covers the canvas with one color. Then He adds smaller splotches of colors. He adds definition with the new colors He's never used before. It takes Him a long time to create this piece so that it is distinctly different from others and yet has similarities to past paintings. When it's finally done, He's very pleased. He puts His thumbprint in the upper left corner. There—it's marked with His signature as His creation. And it is perfect in His sight.

So it is with you. You were created perfect in His sight, by Him and for Him. His thumbprint is upon your heart as a seal of ownership of your spirit and soul.

The Bible lists numerous names for the almighty God. Each has an artistic and creative component. He is the "Author of Life," of *your* life, meaning He has thought about and written every word there is to know about who and what you are. He is the "Master Craftsman." You were hand-crafted, gently chiseled with delicate care. He is the "Potter." Each of your features, inside and out, were formed and molded by His sensitive fingertips. He is the "Father." Every living thing was created by Him.

We feel it's important that you really understand how important you are to God. You didn't happen by accident; you weren't born by mistake. God creates every life, yours included. Your life matters greatly to Him.

6

H-U-G
Yourself

Okay, so you agree and believe God is the author and cre-
ator of your life and body. But maybe that doesn't make you
feel any better right now. Maybe you're wondering how
God is involved in the development of your body.

ELLEN

*I know God made me to be me. And I'm sure, or so my mom
says, there is a reason why I am the way I am. But I still want
to know, why did He have to make me fat? What purpose can it
possibly be serving? If I was skinny, or at least thinner, I'm sure
I'd be a better Christian.*

Have you too questioned the wisdom of the way God created you. We believe the answers to "why" lie in accepting
who and how you are *now*. Remember you are *developing*.
This means you are not the final product yet. It means God
is still working on you, and He has a very definite plan for
your body and life. While this process is going on, it's easy
to become frustrated and impatient. But you need to learn
to like and appreciate yourself and your body now. You
need to learn to hug yourself. "Hug myself?" you may ask.

"How?" Think about the H-U-G guideline: H = Human, U = Ultimate, and G = Gorgeous. Let us explain what we mean.

H = HUMAN

Remember Genesis 1:27, which tells how God created man and woman as *human beings* in His image? Not plants, animals, or insects. Humans. Why? Because He wanted fellowship, someone with whom He could share His creation. Because He wanted a living, breathing, *thinking* creature who could offer Him companionship and praise. Human beings are the pinnacle and highest point of His creation.

IT IS A PRIVILEGE TO BE A HUMAN BEING!

U = ULTIMATE

As we said at the beginning of this chapter, you are in a *refining* process. Refining means getting better and becoming more Christlike. You are in the process of *becoming.* Becoming what? Becoming a young woman of God who will develop into a woman of God. Second Corinthians 1:21-22 says, "He anointed us, set his seal of ownership on us, and put his *Spirit in our hearts as a deposit, guaranteeing what is to come"* (emphasis ours). Also read 2 Corinthians 3:18: "And we, who with unveiled faces all reflect the Lord's glory, *are being transformed into his likeness with ever-increasing glory,* which comes from the Lord, who is the Spirit" (emphasis ours). "Guaranteeing what is to come" and "being transformed" both speak of an ongoing action, a process by which you may:

ULTIMATELY BECOME THE SPIRITUALLY GIFTED FEMALE
THAT GOD DESIGNED EVERY WOMAN TO BE

G = GORGEOUS

Because you were created in the image of God, you can't help but be gorgeous. God isn't ugly, is He? No, God is the essence of beauty. He created all beauty. And you are part of His creation. At this stage in your life, you may feel awkward and unsightly. But as we said in the "ultimate" category, you are still becoming gorgeous. Even so, you are God's child, His princess, trying on queenly qualities, attitudes, and roles to prepare you to become the gorgeous final product He has in mind for you. Look at Psalm 45:13-15: "All glorious is the princess within her chamber; her gown is interwoven with gold. In embroidered garments she is led to the king; her virgin companions follow her and are brought to you. They are led in with joy and gladness; they enter the palace of the king." This princess is like you:

"GLORIOUS" WITH YOUR GOLDEN INNER SOUL,
PREPARING TO COME BEFORE GOD, YOUR KING

GOD IS WATCHING OVER YOU

Have you ever seen a mother cat or dog with a litter of babies? She cuddles each one and noses them toward her belly to eat. She licks their entire bodies to keep them clean. They nestle against her side for warmth. If they cry for her, she comes to them, and after being away, she touches each nose, counting to make sure they are all there. She fusses over them, tenderly caring for and loving each baby.

Zephaniah 3:17 puts these same thoughts into words, telling how God watches over and takes care of you. "He will take great delight in you, he will quiet you with his love, he will rejoice over you with singing."

This is why you need to H-U-G yourself. Because God feels so strongly about your worthiness, about your progress in becoming a gorgeous woman of God, that He rejoices over you even now, *especially now* when you may be feeling less than attractive.

WHAT MAKES YOU *YOU*?

Beyond learning to H-U-G yourself, we want to help you like yourself, to help you develop a deeper understanding of yourself and what makes you *you*.

You each have things that you find interesting or things you like to do. Ellen likes to draw; Betsy likes to play sports. Use the following list or make a list in your diary of your areas of interest. Make three columns at the top of a page with these headings. Write at least three to five things under each heading.

Things I Like to Do:

_____

_____

_____

Things I Do Well:

_____

_____

_____

Things I'd Like to Learn to Do:

_____

_____

_____

We'll give you an example. Sara's list might look something like this:

Things I Like to Do:
   Talk to my friends; Go shopping; Go to parties

Things I Do Well:
   Match clothes; Be a friend; Math and history

Things I'd Like to Learn to Do:
   Keep my room organized; Draw; Water ski

Make your own list. What you like to do and what you do well may overlap—that's okay. But write at least three things under each category.

Do you see how this list shows your uniqueness? Lori's list would be completely different from Sara's. Lori likes to spend time alone, reads well, and would like to learn to ride a horse. These likes, and consequently dislikes, make up who you are. They give you and others a sense of who you are. In other words, they help define you. You know what a definition is—a detailed description of something. Your hobbies and interests help explain who you are.

Now you can expand on what you like and what you want to learn to do. This will give you a deeper sense of purpose or direction in your life. Developing an area of interest will give you something to look forward to, a reward, a purpose to hold on to when you may be feeling down.

ELLEN

I collect charms for my charm bracelet. My dad travels sometimes for his job, and once in a while I get to go with him. I've bought charms for my bracelet from the different places he has taken me. I also try to find ones that have some sort of meaning for me. I found one last year that had a tiny paint palette and paintbrush, and, being an artist, I thought it'd go well with my other charms. I like collecting charms. Each little token reminds me of something special or exciting that happened in my life. I'm probably gonna have to buy a new bracelet soon. The one I have is getting too full. But I'd love to start a whole new one. It's like collecting, holding, and touching pieces of my life. And when I start to feel bad about how my body looks right now, the charms help me remember what is important to me.

If you don't already have a hobby or interest that makes you feel good about being you, think about developing one. If you tend to be an organized person, maybe a collection of some sort sparks your interest—stamps, jewelry, old books, postcards, rocks, etc. Or maybe something with a theme—perhaps angels, stuffed cows, airplanes, Noah's arks . . . Be creative! Or maybe instead of a collection, a hobby or activity sounds more interesting—boating, bicycling, writing, drawing, hiking, knitting. All it takes to start a collection is one piece and the desire to find more, and all it takes to pursue a hobby is to start doing it! Pick something, write it down in your journal, and promise yourself to try it for a few weeks or a month. The great thing about your interests is that you can change them whenever you want to! The deeper you get into each interest, or each new one you pursue, the better understanding you will have of yourself. And you know the best benefit of that? You'll really start to like yourself. The more you like yourself, the more confidence you'll have, which will in turn increase your self-esteem.

You know what your self-esteem is. It is what you think of yourself. If you like yourself and who you are, you have a good or high self-esteem. If you dislike yourself and think that you aren't very good at anything, you have a poor or low self-esteem. We want you to develop a high self-esteem.

As you learned in the last chapter, the Lord also holds you in high esteem. You are extremely valuable to Him. Because of His plans for you and His desire to see you grow into a godly woman, He wants you to have confidence in yourself. Through the suggestions in this book, like the lists in this chapter, you will gain self-esteem and self-confidence. It's like a savings account. The more money you invest, or in this case the more time you spend on developing yourself, the larger the profits, or self-esteem, you will gain.

7

What's Inside?

As you learn to like yourself on the outside, with the gifts and skills God has given you, let's take a look at the inside of your body.

Remember Psalm 139, the part that says, "You knit me together?" Can you see God sitting in His huge rocker "knitting" you? The reason the psalmist chose the word *knit* was because our inward parts are so complex and so delicately constructed that it is as if God took a pair of tiny knitting needles and put us together stitch by stitch.

MEN AND WOMEN ARE DIFFERENT

Men and women are both created with sex organs. These are the parts of their bodies that make them distinctly male or female. You know what we mean—boys and men have *penises*; girls and women have *vaginas*. But there is more to it than that.

The sex organs are located on both the inside and outside of a person's body. A man's sex organs are made up of his penis on the outside of his body and his *testicles*, which are inside a sack of skin called the *scrotum* behind his penis. The purpose of testicles is to make and store *sperm*. Millions and millions of them. During intercourse with a woman, millions of tiny single-celled sperm are released from the man's

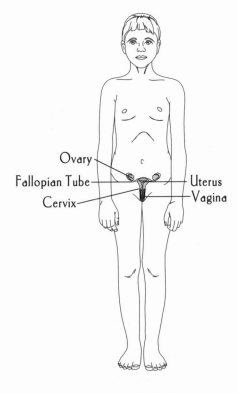

Ovary

Fallopian Tube

Cervix

Uterus

Vagina

Front View
7-A

body. When a sperm cell joins with an *ovum* (egg) cell inside a woman's uterus, the two cells create a new group of living cells. Safe inside the woman's *uterus*, these cells grow and multiply and form into a human baby.

Part of God's purpose for the female body is to have babies. Each female sex organ was created to help bring new life into the world. Each part of a female's body has a specific job, and they all must work together to produce a child.

This isn't to say every woman should or will have children. Some wives and husbands choose not to have a child. Other married couples can't; their bodies aren't able to pro-

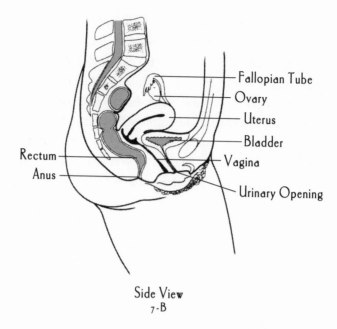

Fallopian Tube
Ovary
Uterus
Bladder
Rectum
Vagina
Anus
Urinary Opening

Side View
7-B

duce children. We know you aren't even thinking about babies yet, but it is important for you to understand how your body functions long before you get married and think about having children.

BETSY

ᕍ

My mom has explained the "facts of life" to me. And even though I've had my period a few times, I still have a lot of questions. For one thing I can't seem to picture what all these "organs" look like in my body. It seems like my body is way too small to have so many "womanly parts" in there. How big are they? How do they all fit?

There are five basic internal organs (or organs inside your body) that make you a woman. These are *ovaries, fallopian tubes, uterus, cervix,* and *vagina.*

To help you "see" this better, for a moment think of your entire body as the female organs. Hold your arms out from your sides with your hands in a fist. Your fists are like ovaries with your arms like the fallopian tubes leading to the uterus, or your upper body. From your shoulders to your waist is like the uterus, ending at your hips. The cervix area would be in the region of your hips to your legs, and your legs represent the vagina. This "model" is very similar to the positioning and connection of these organs inside your body.

Model
7-C

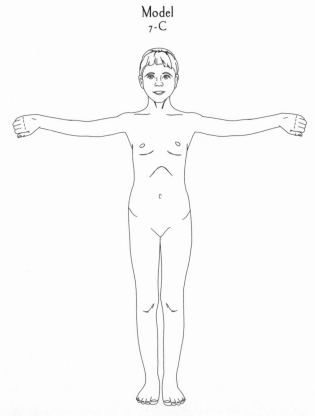

Illustration concept adapted by permission from *A Volunteer Training Manual* by Cynthia Phikill and Suzanne Walsh, published by Frontlines Publishing in 1997.

Deep inside your pelvis, the area between your hips and your vulva (or your *genitals*, the external part of where you go to the bathroom), are the five organs. All together they take up a space about the same size as a teacup. Let's look at each one individually.

The Ovaries

The ovaries are grayish pink and shaped like two small almonds. They are home to many young *ova* or eggs. These eggs can't be seen without a microscope, but they are still the largest cells in a woman's body.

Once you start your periods and have a fairly regular cycle (or pattern of periods), your ovaries release one egg each month. This is called *ovulation*. Ovulation occurs about ten to fourteen days before your period—but don't worry, most young women never feel this when it happens. It's usually painless. When the released ovum becomes *fertilized* (or joined) with sperm from a man, a little human baby begins to grow inside a woman's uterus.

An interesting tidbit about God's design of the female body is that when you were born, you had all the immature eggs your body would ever need already present in your ovaries. That's hundreds of thousands of them! Wow!

Fallopian Tubes

After the egg is released from the ovary, it travels through the hollow fallopian tube. The egg cannot move by itself, but it is moved along by little hairs inside the tube. Like ovulation, the egg's journey is completely painless, and most young women don't know when it's happening. It can take up to two days for the egg to reach its destination—the uterus.

The Uterus

The fallopian tubes connect to the top of the uterus. The uterus (or womb) is a pear-shaped organ about the size of your fist. God made the womb to be home to a growing baby. Each month the uterus waits to see if it needs to nourish a fertilized egg (a tiny growing group of cells that will form into a baby). When there has been no intercourse with a man and therefore no sperm to join with the egg, the unfertilized egg arrives at the uterus. This unfertilized egg will not grow into a baby, so about ten days after the egg arrives, the uterus sheds the egg and some blood. This is called your period, or *menses.*

Some women do feel discomfort during their periods—sort of an achy lower back and low stomach cramps. Generally the uncomfortable feeling lasts only a day or two. We'll talk more about your periods, what to expect, and what they are like in chapter 8.

The Cervix

The cervix is at the lower end of the uterus with a small opening that connects the uterus to the vagina. Touch your finger to your nose—that is how your closed cervix feels—slightly knobby.

God designed the cervix as a way to protect a growing baby from germs and from being born too soon. The cervix is tightly closed except when a woman is about to have a baby. Then the cervix opens enough to allow the baby to pass through.

During your period the blood that is shed from your uterus passes through the cervix and into the vagina. Because the opening of your cervix is small, sometimes there is a little discomfort.

The Vagina

The vagina is the passageway from the cervix to the outside of your body. The vagina doesn't go straight up toward your stomach but angles back toward your lower spine. Its opening is between your *urethra* (where you urinate) and your *anus* (where you pass bowel movements from your *rectum*).

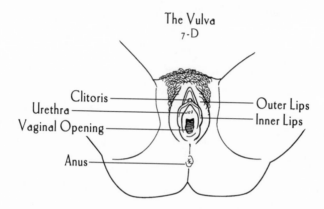

The Vulva
7-D

Clitoris
Urethra
Vaginal Opening
Anus
Outer Lips
Inner Lips

The vaginal canal is about two to three inches long and is made up of very flexible muscles. Usually the canal is narrow, but during childbirth it stretches to allow a baby to pass through.

During your period the discharge from your uterus leaves your body through the vagina. Tampons, which some women use to absorb the blood during their periods, are placed inside the vagina. We'll talk more about tampons in chapter 8.

It's important to know where these parts are in and on your body. They are part of *you*, not separate from you. It's okay and a good idea to use a hand-held mirror to look at your womanly parts. Notice where the placement is of your labia lips, which protect the openings to your urethra and vaginal opening. Your anus is in back of these parts.

Eventually hair will cover most of your vulva, offering even more protection and coverage.

No female part can work well without the others. God made each one of your female organs with a specific purpose—the ovaries to produce an egg; the fallopian tubes to carry the egg; the uterus to house, nourish, and protect the fertilized egg as it grows into a baby; the cervix to protect the baby from illness and being born too soon; and the vagina as the exit from the mother's body for the baby to enter the world. Even though you won't be ready to have a baby until you are married, all the organs you need are already in place. They are what make you distinctly a woman.

First Corinthians 12:18 says, "But in fact God has arranged the parts in the body, every one of them, just as he wanted them to be." Do you feel in awe yet of just how wonderfully God designed you? It is awesome! He is an awesome God, creating every little cell, every invisible piece of your body. God is huge, beyond our imagination; yet He is small enough to gently piece you together into a beautiful and perfectly made young woman!

8

Pause for Periods

SARA

ᨒ

I still don't understand about periods. What makes the egg get released from the ovaries, and why do women bleed every month?

Even though I don't understand it all and feel a little afraid of when it's going to happen to me, I'm fascinated by it too. It seems so secretive, but I want to know all about it. I want it to be a part of my life . . . I think.

The other day I took one of my mom's tampons out of the bathroom. I went into my room and closed the door so I could look at it closer. I took the wrapper off. It looked like two tubes, a small one poking out from the bottom of a big one. I pushed the bottom part of the cylinder up into the bigger one, and out came the tampon. It looked like a long, thick piece of cotton with a piece of string attached to one end. This is supposed to fit into my vagina? It looks like it might hurt.

I think my mom must have found out that I was taking apart the tampon because yesterday she bought me a box of panty liners. She said that when my period starts (When? Please soon!), all I'll need is these because I won't bleed very much the first

*couple of times. I'm glad. I don't think my body is ready for a
tampon.*

Have you given a lot of thought to your period too, like
Sara? Do you wonder when it will start, what makes it happen, and what it's going to be like? We'll try to answer some
of these questions for you.

HORMONES

You know there are various vital organs in your body that
keep you alive—your heart, lungs, brain, kidneys, etc. These
are part of your nervous system, the system that keeps your
body functioning.

Your body also houses the *endocrine* system. This system
helps your body to keep a balance in your growth, development, maturity of your female organs, and use of the food
you eat.

The endocrine system is made up of hormones (when
you are in a bad mood, has your mom ever accused your
"hormones" of putting you in a bad mood?). Hormones are
chemical messengers that talk to various organs throughout
your body. Think of these messengers as little letters
"mailed" from your brain to certain parts of your body.
When the "mail" reaches its destination, the organ opens the
letter, reads the instructions, and performs the task the brain
asked it to do. Some of the "mail" may take just a split second to get to where it's going and trigger a response. Other
times the response may not come for much longer, weeks or
even months. This is why it takes awhile for your body to
develop breasts and start your period. The "mail" is slower
moving from your brain and more gradual in getting a
response from your female parts.

The amount of hormones in your body is constantly

changing because your maturing body hasn't learned how to regulate the levels yet. Even if you don't recognize the different hormones surging through your body, you will feel the effects of the rise and fall of hormones. One minute you may find yourself happy without a care in the world; the next you might be crying over something that never used to bother you. One day you might be ravenously hungry, and the next you might feel bloated and lethargic. These fluctuations are all tied into the rise and fall of hormones in your body. This is all very normal.

Two primary hormone groups change your body from a young girl's to a young woman's body. They are the *estrogens* and *progesterone*. The estrogens in particular work to mature your female organs, starting the ovulation and period cycles, adding fat and muscle around your hips, thickening your breast areas, and growing body hair. Progesterone is more active when your uterus is housing and nurturing a baby.

All the hormones in your body are vital for your well-being, and like every other part of your body, they can't work alone. They each need the presence of the others to work properly. As a spring daffodil poking up through the ground depends on good soil, water, and sunshine to grow into maturity, so your body depends on hormones as one factor in your growth into a woman.

JUST TELL ME WHEN MY PERIOD IS GOING TO START

Okay, okay! We know you are impatient to have your first period. (If you already have started your periods, congratulations! Keep reading this part though.)

If we could predict when your period is going to start, it might not have been necessary for us to write this book! It would've been interesting if God had just said, "On every young woman's thirteenth birthday, she will start her period." But He didn't. You know why? Because He doesn't like to give us too much information at once. It has taken this many years, since the beginning of His created time, for scientists to figure out the workings of the human body. And we still have so much to learn! He wants our bodies to remain something of a mystery. If we knew everything about how our bodies work, we might think we have very little need for God in our lives. He wants us to remain dependent on Him. And He is reminding you through this waiting time that His timing is perfect.

Some young women start their periods at age eleven. Others don't start until they are sixteen. Both ages and anywhere in between is considered average. Even though we can't predict exactly when your period will start, we can say with confidence that it is "in the works" even as you read this sentence.

You may have noticed over the last couple of years that you do have some discharge from your vagina. It's usually pale yellow to almost clear in color. You may notice that the consistency of the discharge changes too. Sometimes it might be thick and kind of clumpy; other times it might be thin, almost stringy. These are normal variations. The discharge tells you that your body is gearing up for your menstrual cycle (periods). Once your periods start, there will even be a pattern to the color and consistency of the discharge.

WHAT WILL MY PERIODS BE LIKE?

Just as Sara's mom told her, your first few periods will be very light and last just a few days. Your first period may catch you off guard at school or out shopping. But don't worry, it's unlikely that it will seep through your clothes. If you carry a backpack or book bag, you could put a couple of panty liners in one of the inside pockets just for your peace of mind.

The first few times you might feel a little cramping, but if you're busy, you might not feel anything. If you do have some discomfort, ask your mom for some acetaminophen or ibuprofen. Either will help to decrease any cramping or pain. But

DON'T TAKE ASPIRIN!

until you are older than sixteen. Aspirin can cause a serious illness in children and young adults. And

NEVER, EVER TAKE MEDICATION FROM ANYONE

other than your parents, school nurse, or physician. You should always ask or tell your mom or dad when you need to take pain medication for period discomfort.

For a few days before your period starts, you might feel bloated and constipated. It's just those hormones again preparing your body to have a period. Some women get a little diarrhea or loose stools at the beginning of their periods too. All of this is normal, and as your periods become more regular, you will begin to recognize these signs as a warning that your period is about to start that month.

Likely, the way you'll know you have started your period the first time is that the toilet tissue will appear a little pink or light red after you have gone to the bathroom. Early periods are generally pink-tinged mucus, not bright red blood like what you would see if you cut your hand. The mucus will change in color as your period starts to go away. It may change to a rust color or even brownish. Again this is very normal. The darker color is just a sign that the last of the blood in your uterus is being shed.

Period Cycles

Initially, your periods will last only two to three days. As you get older, they may increase up to a full seven days. Some women have their periods for just three days every month; other women may bleed for seven days every six weeks. Anything in between these two boundaries is normal.

Your periods will be very irregular for about the first year. You may have one period a month for three months and then not have a period at all for two months. Or you may go as much as six months in between the first couple of periods. Usually within two years a pattern has formed.

This pattern of your period is called your *menstrual cycle*. The cycle actually starts on the *first* day of your period and ends on the day that your period starts again. When your period ends, your body goes through a resting phase. Then about ten to fourteen days later, your ovaries produce a mature egg, and you ovulate. Another ten to fourteen days pass, and your period begins. Your body sheds blood for three to seven days. Then the cycle starts all over again. Most women's menstrual cycles range from twenty-eight days to forty days.

Feminine Protection

As your menstrual cycle becomes more regular, the flow (or the amount of blood you pass) during your period will increase. As Sara's mom suggested, all you'll need at first is panty liners to protect your underwear. But eventually you will need more protection. You'll need to switch to mini-pads or even maxi-pads. Pads and tampons are also called "feminine protection." Your mom can help you pick out which kind is best for you.

Using a mini-pad or panty liner is easy. One side of the pad is a soft cottonlike material. The other side is sticky— usually with a paper strip covering it. The soft side goes against your body. The sticky side sticks to the narrow crotch part of your underwear.

Some women find pads bulky, with possible leakage around the edges of the pad. A tampon is less likely to leak. Sara found out that tampons look a little scary, but when inserted into the vagina properly, they shouldn't hurt. Anyone can wear them, but you might want to start with the slender kind designed specifically for young women. Again, ask your mom to help you pick out the ones that will suit you best.

Inside of each box of tampons are detailed instructions and pictures of how to insert a tampon into your vagina. It may take several tries. You may feel some pressure when you first try them, but it shouldn't hurt to insert one. After the tampon is inserted correctly, two to three inches of the string will hang down between your legs. When it's time to change your tampon, a gentle tug on the string will pull it out. If for some reason the string gets pushed up into your vagina, you can insert a clean finger into your vagina to reach the string or tampon and pull it out. Because of your tightly closed cervix, the tampon cannot travel up into your uterus—in other words, a tampon cannot "get lost" inside your body!

You'll want to change your panty liner or pad at least every four hours. You may need to change it more often as you get older and your flow gets heavier. Don't flush used tampons or pads down the toilet. They can stop up the plumbing! Wrap them in toilet tissue and put them in the trash.

Tampons need to be changed about every four hours

also and should not be worn overnight. A dangerous illness called toxic shock syndrome (TSS) has been associated with having a tampon inside your body for too many hours. This is a bacterial infection that causes flulike symptoms—fever, nausea, and vomiting, dizziness, headache, all-over aches, rash, etc. If you have these symptoms when you are using tampons, tell your mom or dad, and call the doctor immediately. The package insert in a tampon box also can give you more detailed information about TSS.

BETSY

I remember my first period kinda scared me. I was standing in front of the mirror putting my hair into a ponytail to keep it out of my face for softball practice. I was gonna go to the bathroom before I left, but all of a sudden it felt like I'd wet my pants a little. I went into the bathroom and saw a little pink stuff on my underwear. I knew right away it was my period, but somehow I'd expected it to be more bloody—redder, or something. I thought it'd be like a stream, sorta gushing out of me 'cause Mom kept calling it a "flow," but it was barely a trickle. I stuck one of those panty liners on my underwear and went to softball practice. When I ran from base to base, it felt like I had this thin piece of cardboard in my underwear, but after a while I got used to it. I switched to tampons the next time I got my period though. They're more comfortable for playing sports.

Now, six months after that first period, I look in the mirror and wonder if I look different. Can people tell I've started menstruating? Mom calls it a "rite of passage." I think she means I've passed from girlhood into womanhood, and I guess in a way I look at myself more as a young woman now. But I'm still a great softball player!

9

What's Outside?

We have just finished talking about your period and what's going on inside your body—none of which is visible to anyone looking at you. Oh, they might notice your facial features taking on a more mature look or your hips widening a bit, but others can't see your female parts "ticking like clockwork," marking your journey into womanhood.

What does become more noticeable around the same time you start your periods is the development of your breasts. Maybe you already feel a thickening in your breast area, or your nipples seem to be getting bigger and darker in color. It's those hormones again, those little mail messengers from your brain telling your breasts to grow.

God designed breasts as a way to provide food for a baby. Like all mammals that have mammary glands, women's breasts produce milk to feed growing babies. When a woman is pregnant, different hormones from her brain are released telling her breasts to make and store milk. When a baby is born, he or she knows instinctively how to nurse, or suck on the mother's breast for food. The more the growing baby nurses, the more milk the mother's breasts produce. A woman can nurse her baby for several months without feeding him or her any other food. God's design of the human breast to supply food is perfect for a baby's nutritional needs. Many mothers consider breast milk a baby's "birthing right."

Why do we want you to understand the real purpose of a woman's breast? Because the culture we live in has made us forget that breasts have a God-given purpose. You've seen TV ads, billboard signs, or ads in magazines that show women with large breasts. These ads are trying to say that women with large breasts are prettier or more appealing. We know that's not true! That's being prejudiced!

ELLEN

Because I'm on the heavy side, I have, as my mom calls them, "young women's breasts." She just bought me a real bra, not one of those training things that's just like a halter top. I kinda like it. It makes me feel grown up. But my little sister Marsha teased me the other day. She's so stu . . . well, I'm not supposed to say that word. Let's just say she's really silly. She thought because I was wearing a bra, I had milk in my breasts! I know you don't get milk until you have a baby, but Marsha kept pushing one of her baby dolls into my chest saying, "You want to nurse the baby?" I got so irritated at her, I wanted to scream. Mom heard us fighting, and when she found out what my sister was saying, Mom took Marsha into her bedroom and closed the door. I listened outside the door and heard Mom tell Marsha about girls' breasts. Marsha asked when she would grow hers. I didn't hear what Mom said 'cause I was laughing too hard. My little sister with breasts—now that's a funny picture!

Maybe like Ellen's little sister, you are wondering when your breasts will grow. Or maybe you're already wearing a bra of some sort. Perhaps your breasts are already so big you're kind of embarrassed by them, and you wear big shirts to hide them. Whatever the stage of your breast growth, you probably feel a little shy about them, especially if you are being teased. It is good to feel modest about protecting your breasts and body. It's actually biblical. In Genesis 3:7, after Eve and Adam ate the fruit of good and evil, sinning against God's strict orders, they realized they were naked and became shy about their nakedness. "Then the eyes of both of them were opened, and they realized they were naked; so they sewed fig leaves together and made coverings for themselves." Modesty about the body and the desire to keep private parts covered is God-given, since Adam and Eve fell into sin in the garden.

Everyone's breasts will develop at different times. Maybe yours have started, like Ellen's, or maybe you're still very undeveloped. It's not fair to compare yourself with your friends or even with other members of your family. Remember in chapter 5 where we talked about how God designed you as you? He made us each uniquely different because He has an unlimited ability to create new and different people! Imagine how boring this world would be if we all looked the same.

To make matters even more interesting, sometimes a young woman's two breasts grow at different rates. Your right breast might be smaller than your left for a while. Very often your right breast if you're right-handed, or your left breast if you're left-handed, will be larger than the other breast. Uneven growth is normal. This unevenness of breast size is most noticeable to you, looking down onto your chest. If you look in a mirror, it isn't so obvious. Be assured, your breasts will even out and be about equal size eventually. In the meantime, wearing loose-fitting shirts will make it less noticeable to others.

WHAT ABOUT BRAS?

Bras, or brassieres, are meant to support your breasts. Some women like the feeling of support, especially if they are very active. Other women prefer not to wear a bra at all. Your own comfort will decide what you want to wear.

The sizes of bras are determined by the circumference of your chest, which is an even number. The cup size of your breasts is a letter. These numbers together are also called your "bust line." A small person like Betsy will have a small measurement such as 26 or 28. A larger person like Ellen might be a size 34 or 36. These are the "band" measurements. The "cup" size is the actual size of your breasts. The smallest cup size is AAA. The largest is a DD/E. An A cup is fairly small, just a little swell of breast tissue. The middle cup sizes are B, C, and D. You will likely mature to a B or C cup. This is the average size of most women's breasts. Bras are sized according to these two measurements. An average five-foot, six-inch woman would probably wear a bra size of 36B. Because Betsy is small, her bra size might be a 26A. Ellen's might be a 34B.

If you choose not to wear a bra during your breast-growing years, you might want to wear loose T-shirts. They don't offer any support, but they do help to protect your modesty. Your mom can help you decide what is right for you. We know, this might be another one of those embarrassing times when you wish you didn't have to talk about your body with your mom. But, trust us, she really cares about your concerns, and she wants to help you through this time of shyness about your developing breasts.

If you don't want to go to a store with your mom to pick out bras, ask her to do it for you. A way to help her decide what size to get for you is to measure your bust line. Take a tape measure and put it around your back to meet in the front of your body right below your breasts. If this number is an even number, add four inches to it. If it's an odd number, add five inches to it. This number in inches will give you the first number we talked about, the "band" measurement—28, 30, 32, etc. So if your measurement was 25, add five inches to get a band measurement of 30. Or if your measurement was 24, add four inches to give you a 28-inch band.

Then you need to decide on the cup size. If your whole hand can cover your breast area and your fingers end up under your armpit, then you probably need an AA or A cup. If your breast takes up more of your palm, you might need a B cup. Another way to find out what size cup you need is to take the tape measure again, and this time have the ends of the tape measure meet across the largest part of your breasts. If the measurement is about the same as the first band number, you'll need an AA or A cup. If it's one inch bigger, you'll need a B cup, two inches bigger a C cup, etc.

Measurement #1

9-A

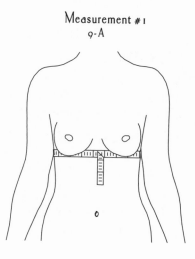

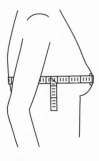

Measurement #2
9-B

It may seem a little strange to touch yourself for these measurements. But we want you to be comfortable with your body. That means you need to touch yourself sometimes. You also can look at yourself in the mirror and study different parts of your body. It's your body! Get to know it by touching it and looking at it. This is part of becoming comfortable with its growth.

OTHER BODY DEVELOPMENTS

You may also have started to notice hair growing on your vulva, or your groin area. *Pubic* hair, as it is called, is another sign that hormones from your brain are telling your body to become a woman. We believe God designed this hair as a form of protection for your delicate parts, your genitals, and also as a covering of modesty. As you get older, the few hairs you see now will thicken and indeed hide your female parts. Your pubic hair may be curly or straight and may be the same color as the hair on your head or a very different color.

Shaving

You may also notice that the hair on your legs, arms, and underarms is getting darker and thicker. Some young women like to start shaving their legs and armpits as soon as their body hair gets dark. Blonde or light-haired women tend to have finer, lighter-colored body hair and don't need to shave often or very soon in adolescence. Dark-haired girls may need to shave more frequently because their body hair is also dark. Redheads frequently have blonde body hair and can sometimes get away with not shaving at all.

Initially it might be safest to use a small rechargeable electric razor until you get the hang of shaving over curves and bones. Your flesh is very delicate, and a razor can cut painfully deep. Like men who shave their faces consistently, the more you shave your legs and underarms, the more often you will have to do it because the more you shave, the more the hair grows.

NEVER, EVER BORROW ANYBODY'S RAZOR!

Even from another family member. Razors can and frequently do make tiny cuts in the skin. Tiny amounts of blood are then on the blade. Anything that has blood on it— whether you can see it or not—should never be used by other people, because germs from the blood can then be passed to the next person.

LORI

I tried shaving my legs last month. The hair on my legs looked dark and yucky to me. It stuck straight up when I had the goose bumps during gym at school. I thought I saw one of the other girls staring at my legs. I was so embarrassed I just wanted to get rid of all that hair! I took a bath as soon as I got home from school and tried to use one of my dad's disposable razors while I was in the tub. Man, did I hurt myself! I got little nicks all over my bony legs, and did they sting! I had to wear long pants for a while to cover up all those cuts.

Dad got mad at me 'cause I used one of his razors. It's not like he didn't have other ones! He told me not to touch his razors again, and then he said I was too young to be shaving my legs anyway. I went to my room and cried. I was just trying to get rid of that stupid hair. Doesn't he see I'm growing up and not just a little girl anymore? Why couldn't he just leave me alone?

Mom came in and apologized and said she would talk to him about my not being a little girl anymore. Good! Does he want me to stay a little girl forever? She said no, that it's just hard for him to think of me as a young woman. I guess I can understand that. It's hard for me to think of myself as a woman. She also said she knows I want to start shaving, so she'll buy me an electric razor. She said I'll like it better anyway.

If you choose to shave with a disposable razor, mark it as yours with tape or water resistant marker. While in the tub or shower, lather your legs or underarms with soap. Without too much pressure, shave *up* your legs and *down* your armpits. If you do nick yourself, place a small piece of tissue on the area for a few minutes to help it stop bleeding.

KEEPING YOUR BODY CLEAN

With the rise in hormones and the growth of underarm hair comes body odor. Also known simply as BO, the sweat from your body begins to take on a distinctly unpleasant smell.

You have always had sweat glands in your body; you were born with them. But as you mature, the glands become more active in ridding your body of toxins. These poisons are released through perspiration, or sweat. You may have already noticed that sometimes if you eat really greasy foods or heavy spicy foods that you can smell the odor on yourself the next day. Those odors, along with sweat produced from normal daily activities, may leave you feeling a little smelly.

There are several things you can do to get rid of body odors. Bathing at least every other day with a deodorant soap will help. Taking a shower versus a bath is a personal decision. Some girls prefer showers over baths because in a bath they feel as if they are sitting in dirty water. Others prefer baths because they feel that a good soak is what gets them clean. Either choice is fine.

During your period you might want to wash everyday. Keeping your vulva and genitals, your private parts area, clean is very important all the time, but especially during your period. Some women do notice a smell toward the end of their periods because the discharge is "old."

You should wipe yourself after using the bathroom from the front of your privates toward the back, from your urethra, where you urinate, toward your anus, where you have bowel movements. Wiping the other way around, back to front—from your anus toward your vagina and urethra—could bring normal bacteria that is around your anus into your vaginal opening or into your urethra. This bacteria can cause uncomfortable infections.

You can also start using an underarm deodorant every day. A deodorant coats your underarms and prevents the smell from getting through. You can even start using it before you notice any body odor, just so you get in the habit of using it every day.

Around the time your periods start, you may have an increase in facial blemishes too. Pimples or zits are blocked skin pores. Pimples aren't limited to just your face. Some people get them all over their bodies, especially on their backs. Teenagers seem to be more prone to blemishes than other people because their bodies are still trying to regulate their hormones, glands, and metabolism (the body's use of food). Some people have more trouble with pimples than other people.

One way to decrease pimples is to limit how much greasy or fatty foods you eat. Yes, we know, there's nothing quite so yummy as a burger and fries or pizza, but eating greasy foods definitely increases your chances of getting pimples. It's okay to have fries or pizza occasionally but not every day. (We'll talk more about the foods you eat in chapter 10). Also washing your face every day with a cleanser that is specifically for blemish-prone people can help.

SEEING A DOCTOR

We can't stress enough the importance of having a yearly checkup with your doctor. God has entrusted you with this incredible gift, your body. Part of your respect for yourself and the gift He has given you is to care for it properly. And that care includes yearly checkups to make sure your growth and development are progressing well. Many schools require annual physicals as do sports teams and camps.

Yearly checkups are sort of like what you have to do with a car. You know that your parents have to put the right gas in the car, change the oil, check the tires, add windshield wiper fluid, take the car in for regular maintenance, etc. Your body is the same way. It needs constant maintenance and upkeep to make sure it is working right and will continue to run well.

Your mom probably still schedules these appointments for you. Maybe you already see a female doctor or nurse practitioner, but if you don't, you might ask your mom if you could switch to a woman. You'll probably feel more comfortable, especially as you get older, discussing your health concerns with another woman. She will better understand your feelings and will be able to answer any questions you have about your body. A female doctor probably remembers what it was like to be your age, and you may find her easy to talk to.

With all these external changes you can see that God really likes to keep you on your toes, doesn't He? He wants you to have feelings of anticipation about your body. He wants you to be interested in the development of your womanly parts. The wonder and excitement you feel about your growing body *pleases God*. Why? Because you are His creation, and He loves for His creation to be appreciated and respected. It pleases Him when people give Him thanks for their lives and bodies.

When you were younger, you liked it when your mom and dad watched you dance around the living room or they taped on the "fridge" every picture you drew? You wanted to show off your abilities, your creations, for your mom and dad to admire and appreciate. That's how the Lord feels. He wants to show off His creation—*you*. And, even more, He wants you to love how you were made!

10

Keeping Track

BETSY

Since I've started my period, I keep expecting it every month, but it hasn't been happening that way. The first time it came was on the fifteenth of the month. I remember because it was the softball game when I got a home run. I guess my period didn't slow me down too much that day! But now I keep thinking my period will come back on the fifteenth every month, but it doesn't. Mom says my cycle will get more regular as I have more periods, but I wish I could predict each month when it's gonna happen so I'd be prepared.

There will be a pattern for your menstruation cycle eventually. But the first couple of years it can be hit or miss. This may drive you nuts—feeling fearful it could catch you off guard someplace. As we suggested earlier, you might carry panty liners with you always, just for your peace of mind.

Even though you may not have started your periods yet, or if you've just had a few, it's a good idea to keep track of them. You might wonder, *If I haven't had any yet, how am I supposed to keep track of them?* Let us explain.

After your mom reads *Just for Moms,* she'll want to buy a calendar for you. As you know from the previous chapters, your womanly health is far more than just your periods. It's your entire bodily health. It's what you think, your relationship with the Lord, what you eat, how you exercise, your personal interests, your relationship with your family, and the care of your body. Womanly health is, simply, your lifestyle. *My lifestyle? How?*

PUTTING IT ALL TOGETHER

Remember in chapter 4 where we talked about the importance of keeping a journal or diary? We hope you've started writing down your daily feelings, your emotions about what's going on in your life. The journaling you've been doing now needs to start including your physical health too.

On a small calendar that is either part of your journal or separate from it, you'll want to start writing down any vaginal discharge you have. We talked about this a little in chapter 9. The discharge might be clear or yellow, or you may have nothing at all. A discharge is proof of hormones working inside your body and evidence that your body is gearing up for your periods. On the days you do notice any discharge, make a note of it on your calendar. You could make up a little code and just use initials to write on the calendar. For example, on a day when you have no discharge you could just make a "Z" for zero discharge. On a day when it seems clear and sort of runny, you could write the letters "CL" and "R." Just make note and remember what the initials stand for! We call this "tracking" your cycle or the pattern of the rise and fall of your hormones.

Pennies for Periods

Once you start your periods, try this activity to help you keep track of them. We call it "Pennies for Periods."

Ask your mom for or collect the following:

Forty pennies

Ten nickels

Ten dimes

Two business-sized envelopes, one marked with a large green "C," the other blank.

Two smaller envelopes. Mark one of the smaller envelopes with a large yellow "O" and the other with a large pink "P."

Place all the coins in the unmarked business envelope. On the first day of your period, write the date on the back of the envelope with the pink "P" and put a dime in the envelope. For each day of your period put a dime in that envelope. When your period stops, write the date next to the first date and put a penny in the large business envelope marked with a green "C." Every day put a penny in the "C" envelope until you think you might be ovulating. Write the date of the first day that you start ovulating on the back of the small envelope with the yellow "O." Place a nickel in this envelope every day that you are ovulating. When your body returns to little or no vaginal discharge, write the date again next to the first date on the back of the "O" envelope and begin putting a penny a day in the large envelope until you begin your period again. Ask your mom to help you with this activity if it seems a little confusing at first. A bonus to tracking your periods this way might be to put the change in the bank each month and get new coins from your mom or dad for each new cycle.

Using the "Pennies for Periods" method helps you to see

your cycle as well as write about it. Remember, your cycle starts at the beginning of your period and ends at the beginning of your next period.

What's the purpose of all this tracking? Because over time, if you're fairly consistent in writing everything down, you'll see a pattern develop. You might not see a pattern for several months or even a year, but keep at it. A pattern will develop.

This pattern will tell you a lot about your body and what is happening inside when you start to compare it with your written journal. You might notice around the end of every month you have a clear vaginal discharge and at the same time you feel rather irritable. Or maybe you find that when you have no discharge, you tend to be in very happy moods.

It may seem sort of silly to be so in tune with your body, especially where you might not even feel like a young woman yet. If this seems overwhelming to try to keep track of everything now, mark this page and come back to it in six months or so. Continue reading this section though!

Part of the purpose of using a calendar to keep track now is so that when your periods do start, you will already be in the habit of recording your body's workings. Once your periods start, and you faithfully record them, you'll again see a pattern emerge. When you can begin to see the pattern, you can start to predict your entire menstrual cycle every month. And this prediction will give you a feeling of more control over your body. Once you understand the little quirks of your female functioning, your body will seem less foreign to you and more your friend. Remember you're in a partnership with your body—not a war! And that partnership is working together to produce a godly woman.

The pattern of hormonal changes connected with your moods doesn't give you permission to blame your body for a lousy attitude though. Quite the contrary. Since you can now predict when you may have "down" days, you can make other changes so the down days don't seem quite so bad.

But, you may be thinking, *I don't just have down days. It seems that my moods jump all over the place from hour to hour, even minute to minute!* Well, let's take a look at that.

YOU ARE WHAT YOU EAT

You've heard this saying before: "You are what you eat." So does that mean if you eat a lot of sugar, you'll be really sweet? Wouldn't that be nice? Then we could just eat cake and ice cream all day! Unfortunately the saying means that you will experience and live out the *effects* of what you eat. Since we're on the subject of sugar, we'll start there. Sugar—what's in candy bars, chocolate, cake, ice cream, etc.—is a simple carbohydrate. Your body needs carbohydrates to give you energy and strength. But the simple carbohydrates sugar gives your body are just a quick blast of energy. Then they bottom out, leaving you with less energy than before. Sugars can give you a headache and a stomachache and make you tired and cranky and lower your ability to concentrate. It's like a balloon that you blow air into, but then as soon as you let the air sputter out, the balloon shrivels up and becomes lifeless. That's what a sugary candy bar does to your body. At first it fills you up, giving you energy, but then the energy starts to "leak" out of your muscles, leaving you with less energy than you had before.

The other type of carbohydrates are complex carbohydrates. These are found in milk, pasta, rice, grains, fruits, etc. These carbohydrates will give you a slower and longer-lasting boost of energy. They are considered "good" carbohydrates.

Why do we want you to know about carbohydrates?

Because they will have a direct effect on your mood. That's right—what you eat has the ability to put you in a good mood or a bad mood. So why don't we just eat things that keep us in good moods? Because many of us are born with a sweet tooth, we all crave sweet things. But those same sweets are what can make you cranky.

With the rise of hormones in your body, you need to be especially careful about how much sugar you eat. The combination of hormones and sweets can send you right into a terrible mood. During your hormonal cycles, you may crave certain foods. It's okay to have a little of what you crave. Some women want chocolate foods right before their periods. It's okay to have one candy bar, but it's not okay to have three bowls of chocolate ice cream.

Another food sensitivity involves caffeine, found in colas, chocolate, tea, and coffee. Caffeine can give you a headache and make you have a hard time falling asleep. Some women also crave salty foods during a part of their cycles. Salt will increase water retention, the full, bloated feeling in your lower stomach. Other women desire fatty foods, such as chips or pizza. We mentioned earlier that fatty foods can make your skin oily and set you up for pimples. Also fatty foods are not healthy for your heart.

Now this isn't to say you have to eliminate all these foods from your diet. You just need to be careful of how much of them you eat. It's called moderation. Give in a little to your cravings, but don't go overboard.

This is another time you can write in your journal. Record what foods you have eaten and what you crave. Then compare it with your hormonal cycle on your calendar. You will again see a pattern of cause and effect. For example, you might find that you crave chocolate right before you notice a clear stringy vaginal discharge, but after you eat a lot of chocolate you feel irritable and tired. Your body reacted to the chocolate due to the change in hormones that produced the vaginal discharge. Next month you'll know when you see that same type of discharge to avoid chocolate!

Your body isn't done growing yet. You still need to eat foods that your body requires to strengthen bones and muscles. These foods include protein and calcium found in meats and dairy products. Red meat, fish, pork, and chicken all are good sources of protein. Eating calcium-rich dairy products now will help your bones to stay strong in your adult years. You also need lots of fruits and vegetables for essential vitamins and minerals. These help to keep your skin and muscles healthy. Ask your doctor, mom, or physical education teacher to help you find out how much of each of these good foods to eat.

Another important part of your diet is water. Doctors recommend that people drink six to eight glasses of plain water every day. Most people don't drink enough because they wait until they feel thirsty. But by the time you feel thirsty, your body is already short on fluids. You need to drink *before* you feel thirsty. Juices, carbonated water, ice water, lemonade mixes, etc., are all good choices for drinks.

FIT FOR LIFE

Fitness—what does that word mean to you? Running? Swimming? General exercise? Body weight? Gym class? The word *fitness* really refers to your entire body, inside as well as outside.

Fitness of the exterior of your body can mean caring for your skin, hair, and posture. Your skin and hair can get burned and damaged by a lot of exposure to the sun. That doesn't mean you shouldn't go outside though. Actually you need direct sunlight for essential vitamins to keep your body healthy. But the same sun can cause permanent damage to your skin from sunburns. It is very important to protect your skin from burns by using sunscreen with a SPF of 15 or higher every time you'll be in the sun. Sunscreen isn't just for the beach. It's for all outside activities, even winter activities such as skiing! Your mom or dad can help you pick out the right kind for your skin tone and for the part of the country in which you live.

Posture

Have your mom or your teachers told you to sit up straight or stop slouching? We know you get tired of hearing it, but let us explain why they are telling you to correct your posture.

Your body alignment, or the way your feet, knees, hips, shoulders, neck, and head line up, is your posture. Good posture means that if you stand with your side to a full-length mirror, there will be a straight line from your ear to your shoulder, to your elbow, to your hip point, to the back of your knee, to your ankle bone. This is called the "plumb line." When the plumb line is off because of slouched shoulders, over-bent knees, an arched back, or a thrust-forward chin, your whole body, *inside and out*, is affected. How? God designed your body to stand upright. He gave you a backbone, skeleton, and muscles to keep your body straight. But when you don't stay fairly straight, other muscles are pulled out of their normal position. And guess what happens—pain. Do you ever get headaches, backaches, neckaches, stitches in your sides? All of those can be because your body isn't in the plumb line.

Practice getting your body in the right alignment by standing in front of the mirror. Position yourself so an invisible line runs through the points we talked about above. "Memorize" this feel and practice it away from the mirror. After several weeks it will be natural for you to keep your body in this position, and you may find you have fewer headaches, backaches, and neckaches!

Exercise

We would be stopping short of a complete look at your body's workings if we didn't include exercise. We're talking about more than swimming laps or running on a track. Just playing outside, riding a bike, swimming for fun, running around the playground, taking a walk, or even doing house chores such as vacuuming are all forms of exercise.

You know your heart is a muscle. All muscles need to be worked in order to stay strong and healthy as your body continues to grow. Likewise, your heart needs to have a workout. This is called cardiovascular exercise. Your heart beats faster and is getting a workout when you run, bike, swim, etc. Betsy knows what this feels like.

BETSY

When I'm running from base to base at a softball game, my heart is just pounding! I think it's partly because I'm so excited about the game, but it's also because I'm running so fast. I feel as if my heart can't keep up with my legs! Coach says it's good for my heart to beat fast. He tells me I'm exercising my heart. You know what? I can tell when I've exercised and when I haven't. After softball I come home a little tired, but I feel great and usually have a lot of energy the next day. But when we have to cancel a couple of games in a row because of rain, I feel lousy. It's like my body needs the exercise to give me more energy.

Betsy is right—the more you exercise, the more energy you'll have. It seems as if the opposite would be true. But when you exercise, your brain releases *endorphins* (more hormones!). They are your body's "feel-good" chemicals. They actually help your mind to have a better attitude! Exercising also clears your body of built-up toxins from foods you've eaten. When you've been in a bad mood, has your mom ever told you to go take a walk or ride your bike? It's because she knows exercise will likely bring you back in a better mood.

Don't wait to exercise until you're in a bad mood though. Consistent exercise can actually help prevent a bad mood altogether! Riding your bike or taking a walk every day helps your body to maintain a balance in your energy level.

Exercise is another activity you can write in your journal every day. (Your journal is going to get pretty full—great!) Writing down when, how long, and how you exercised every day will add a new piece of information about the pattern of your developing body. And like all the other elements—foods, moods, hormones, and spiritual life (more on your spiritual life in chapter 14), exercise affects every other area of your life.

Try picking a couple of forms of exercise that you could do every day over the next month. What do you like to do? Swim, play tennis, roller skate, walk, or ski? Remember the list from chapter 6 about the things you like to do, do well, and want to learn to do? Use that list to help you decide on a couple of physical activities that you like to do. Decide *today* that you will do one activity each day for at least twenty minutes. After one month we guarantee you will feel a more stable energy level and good attitude. Remember to write your promise to yourself to do the activities in your

journal. If it's written down, you will be more likely to follow through on your promise.

Do you know what you have done over the last chapter?
You've learned to "read" your body. Just as you learned to
read words when you were in kindergarten, you've learned
a new language about your body.

Your body does indeed speak its own language to you.
Do you like mysteries? Well, this new language of your
body is like a mystery. Recording what's happening in your
mind, body, and spirit are the clues to help you learn what
your body is saying. And you are the only one who can
solve the mystery! It's a little scary that you are the only one
who can solve the mystery of how your body is talking to
you, but God, your parents, and this book are also available
to help you. And we can tell you that the solution to the
mystery of your body's language is a real treasure—because
this language is part of what makes you uniquely you.

A Word About Boys

ELLEN

I know I should exercise more. At my doctor's appointment last week, she told me that if I exercised, my weight might stay about the same as it is now, but my body would start to grow up, thinning me out. I do want to try to walk my dog every day. But there's something else—something I've never wanted to admit, and now I'm afraid it's too late.

I've always wanted to play basketball. I like watching basketball games and watching the ball fly through the air. Sometimes it spins; sometimes it looks as if it's still and the rest of the world is just whizzing by it. But I've always wanted to get my hands on a basketball and bounce it, throw it, and shoot it so I can be the one to make it spin. It must be the artist in me, wanting to see and feel the ball moving. I know I'll never play though. I think it's too late now. It's sort of a boy's game, and I sure don't want to play a sport with boys. I know they'll just laugh at me.

Have you felt, like Ellen, a little afraid to play sports, especially "guy sports," and even more especially _in front of_ guys?

As we've said before, there may be times while your body is going through these changes that you want to be alone, to be by yourself and not have to *deal* with anyone, especially boys. Sports or other activities may suddenly seem scary if boys are around. You may feel as if they are staring at you or making fun of you behind your back. Things you used to feel really good at or really enjoyed doing may suddenly lose their appeal because you're afraid boys are watching. Maybe you've given up sports and are filling your time with more reading or inside activities.

The problem is that the boys may really be making fun of you behind your back. It's not because what you're doing is funny-looking or weird. It's because a boy's nature during these same years is to make everything into a joke. Many young men at this age are rude and crude.

Boys mature at a different rate than girls. And it's most noticeable between ages eleven and fourteen. You will be more mature emotionally than boys your age until you are almost twenty. They have a lot of catching up to do by the time they realize that girls are pretty neat and they want to be friends with you. That's why when you are allowed to start dating, you may prefer to be with young men who are a year or two older than you because they will be at about the same maturity level as you.

BOYS AS FRIENDS

Maybe you've grown up with the same boys in your class over the last several years. In grade school you probably played with both girls and boys during recess or in school sports, but maybe lately you've noticed that boys don't want to be near you, and you don't want to be near them. Listen to Lori's story.

LORI

↗

My neighbor Stephen—he's thirteen—and I used to do every-thing together—play house, build forts, climb trees. Then about a year and a half ago, he just stopped wanting to play with me. He didn't want to talk to me at all. He wouldn't even look at me at the bus stop anymore! I felt so sad. I still do. I think even now, so much later, that's why I feel lonely sometimes. I wish if I had done something wrong, he would just tell me.

Dad says Stephen is just ignoring me because he suddenly realized he's a boy and I'm a girl, and he's shy about it. Dad said Stephen doesn't know how to act around me, so he just decided not to talk to me at all. So does that mean he was embarrassed at being my friend? He really hurt me.

Has a similar experience happened to you? A boy you thought was your friend suddenly doesn't even say hello?

Boys often have a harder time with the changes in you than you do. Because they don't have the same emotional maturity to figure things out, they just withdraw and start spending more time with other guys.

They show their uncertainty about how to deal with your changes by teasing you . . . mercilessly. But because they haven't developed much compassion yet, they don't know how or when to stop. Even if you start to cry, they might not stop teasing. It's not very nice of them.

That is the whole issue with boys. They haven't learned how to be nice yet at these ages. Oh, some boys are polite, kind, and respectful because their parents or teachers have taught them to be that way, but left to their own nature, boys won't develop a compassion for others for a few more years. They say what's on their minds with little or no thought about how it will affect others. They just don't consider that what they say could hurt someone.

When boys start to tease you or make fun of you, the best way to make them stop is to ignore them. They *want* you to get upset, cry, stamp your feet, yell, or get mad. If you ignore them, they will stop. Do you have younger brothers, sisters, or cousins? You know that when they are bugging you if you turn and walk away and ignore them, they eventually stop. So it is with boys who bug you. Don't respond to their foolishness, and they will stop bothering you.

Part of the reason boys bother you is because they want to figure you out. And this is just the beginning! Girls and women are a mystery to boys and men. Until they learn how to talk to you *about you*, they try other ways to figure out what makes you laugh, smile, cry, get angry, etc. Teasing is their way of actually saying you *fascinate* them. The more they tease and bug you, the more interested they are in you.

BOYS AND DATING

SARA

The other day on the school bus, Matt, this really cute guy, asked me to sit next to him. The bus was kind of full, and I didn't want to sit way in the back. It gives me a stomachache. Anyway, I sat next to him. He didn't say anything, and neither did I, but I could feel my face getting hot, and when I sneaked a peek at him, he was blushing. It was so cute! Then I started to laugh. I couldn't help it. It just seemed so funny, both of us sitting there with red faces and not talking. But then I think he got mad that I was laughing because he sort of plowed over my legs when he got up to get off at his stop. He'll probably never ask me to sit with him again. But I'd sorta like to, and maybe I'll talk next time.

It's normal to feel a little shy around boys you think are cute. Trust us, the boys feel shy too.

Some of you reading this may already be very interested in boys and thinking about dating soon. The choice of when and if to start dating is one best discussed with your mom and dad.

Dating is a big step in your development, and it shouldn't happen until you and your parents have worked out some guidelines. It's likely they will only let you start dating in groups with other teens and chaperones. It doesn't even have to be called a date, so much as going out with a mixed group of friends. Any guidelines or rules your parents discuss with you are for your protection (also read chapter 13 about staying safe). God has entrusted to your parents the task of raising you to the best of their ability. They are answering to God for their care, discipline, and training of you—something we're sure they don't take lightly! They want you to learn about dating but in a safe environment. Trust the rules they provide for you. These are for your own protection.

WHAT'S HAPPENING IN BOYS' BODIES?

BETSY

ॐ

Because I spend time with guys playing sports, I started wondering about their bodies. It's kind of embarrassing thinking about what's happening in my own body, but I got to wondering if they had some sort of changes like girls do. I've heard them teasing, saying they have their "comma today." But I don't think they really have a monthly thing like girls do.

I got up the courage yesterday to ask Mom what happens to a boy's body at fourteen. She said it's not nearly as dramatic as with girls, but they do have changes going on too.

Boys are going through changes just as you are. They too are taking a trip into adulthood. It's as if both girls and boys are making this journey, but boys are taking a different route. While you, as a young woman, are taking a fairly direct route over the next three to five years or so, boys take a longer, rougher route. It's as if you are taking a plane into womanhood and the boys are taking a slow-moving boat into manhood. Their boat is tossed and smashed by conflicting winds on their difficult course, but when they stay true to the guidelines the Lord provides for them, they arrive at manhood weathered and strong. It just takes longer for them to get to the final destination.

Hormones

Boys have hormones too. The difference is that their main hormone is *testosterone*. Just like what happens in your body, a boy's brain isn't able to regulate the testosterone very well until he gets a little older.

Fluctuating hormones affect a boy's private parts. When his hormones are not in balance or when he sees a pretty girl or has a sexual thought, blood rushes to his penis. The blood pooling in his penis causes it to get hard and bigger. This is called an *erection*. It actually starts happening at a very young age to all boys.

But as boys grow into men, a connection develops between the sexual thoughts they have or things they see (advertisements, pretty women, etc.) and having an erection. It's a boy's body's way of saying, "Hey! That's interesting!" or "Wow! I feel sexually excited by that!" For some young men this can be extremely embarrassing. Sometimes they have frequent erections for no apparent reason. Again, it's the hormones acting in their bodies.

About the same time you are developing breasts and

starting your period, boys bodies also change. They grow pubic hair, underarm hair, facial hair, and some chest hair. Like you, their sweat glands kick into gear, and they start to have body odor. The smell can be quite strong. Generally boys need to start using deodorant before girls.

Boys' voices change around this time. At first a boy's voice will sound kind of crackly, like he has a froggy throat or a cold. But soon a boy's voice drops an octave or two and becomes deeper. It continues to get deeper and thicker in tone until he reaches his late teens.

Just as your period is a sign of your passage into womanhood, to a young man the growth of facial hair is a sign of his passage into manhood. Young men as young as twelve may start shaving, though they probably don't really need to—they just want to. Most young men have significant facial hair, enough to warrant shaving, by the time they are sixteen.

A sometimes embarrassing occurrence for young men is "wet dreams." Technically called *nocturnal emissions*, this happens when the young man has had an erection in his sleep and then a leakage of sperm and fluid from his penis. It may happen when he dreams about a pretty woman. He hasn't wet the bed; the fluid is not urine. He has very little control of these wet dreams, and just as you may be shy about your period, boys do not like to talk about wet dreams. In a young man's case, the wet dreams decrease as he gets older and the testosterone in his body stays steady, whereas with you, your periods will become more regular as your hormones balance out.

MEANT TO BE TOGETHER

Boys, guys, and men—they are God's creations too, and not only His creation but highly esteemed in God's eyes. He created Adam first as the being who would oversee the care of the world, the animals, and his helpmate, Eve. The boys who bother you now will develop into godly men under God's guidance in their lives. They will become loving and sensitive husbands. They will lead honorable lives of integrity. God has a specific and special plan for every young man, just as He has for you.

Men and women were created to be together. Indeed, the Bible says in 1 Corinthians 11:11, "In the Lord, however, woman is not independent of man, nor is man independent of woman." It's hard to imagine right now that God has a mate, a husband, already picked out for you. We know, boys might not be of great interest to you yet. But we also know that is about to change. God's design for males and females is remarkable, awe-inspiring, and frightening all at once!

He has a special plan for you that will someday likely include a man. Right now it's very far off. But in the next chapter we'd like to talk frankly with you about God's awesome design of the male and female body to fit together in sexual unity as one.

Sexual Maturity

This trip you are on through puberty will take you to your final destination of physical maturity. Up to this point we've talked about your developing body as an entity in itself. But God has a plan for your body once it has grown into complete womanhood. The end result of puberty and God's goal for your body is sexual maturity.

We talked about sexual maturity at the beginning of this book as the time when your body is old enough and ready for a sexual relationship with a man. God's perfect plan though is that your sexual relationship will be with just one man for your lifetime—your husband.

WHAT EXACTLY IS A SEXUAL RELATIONSHIP?

God designed all living things with the ability to reproduce—or to make more of their own kind. That is one of His first commands to Adam, Eve, and all of His early creation: "'Be fruitful and increase in number; fill the earth . . . '" (Genesis 1:28). In other words He wants to be sure that everything He created will continue to live. For example, when a male and female cat mate, if the female is at the right point in her heat (or menstrual) cycle, she will become pregnant and in a few short months give birth to kittens. That is

God's design. Males and females will come together to mate and recreate their own kind.

It's a little more complicated in people, however. It's not called "mating," is it? No, the coming together of a man and woman is called many things—sexual intercourse, making love, having sex, having relations, being intimate, and coupling. The word *intercourse* simply means "a place where two things meet." There are other terms too, some that you may have heard, but we feel those are somewhat offensive and don't apply to a husband and wife who make love.

HOW DO A HUSBAND AND WIFE MAKE LOVE?

For people the urge or desire to have sex is very strong. It's those hormones again that are released from a person's brain telling his or her body to seek the pleasure of sexual intercourse. In animals the urge usually happens only during the times the female can get pregnant—maybe twice a year. In humans the urge isn't confined to just those times. Husbands and wives can and do have sex whenever they want. That's because God designed sexual intimacy between a husband and wife to be the ultimate expression of their love for one another.

When a man is aroused, or ready to make love, his penis enlarges and becomes hard—called an erection. When a woman is aroused, her vagina secretes a little fluid, and she has a full feeling in her genitals. Usually the husband and wife are naked and lying in bed. The husband may lie on top of his wife, or they may be side to side, or the wife may lie on top of her husband. The man gently inserts his penis into his wife's vagina. This feels very good to both of them. They move their hips together so that the husband's penis slides in and out of his wife's vagina. They do this rhythmically until a warm, pleasant sensation passes over both of them (called an *orgasm*). When this happens, the man *ejaculates*, meaning that about a teaspoon or so of fluid that contains sperm is released from his penis into his wife's vagina. At about the same time, her vaginal muscles contract and release. If the wife is at the point of ovulation in her menstrual cycle, she may become pregnant from the sperm that her husband released into her vagina.

The time it takes to make love may be just a few minutes to over an hour. It depends on the couple. Most husbands and wives talk about making love—what feels good to their bodies and how it makes them feel emotionally. The whole act is very exciting, pleasing, and intimate to them.

WHY DO HUMANS MAKE LOVE?

As we said earlier, one of the reasons humans have sexual intercourse is to become pregnant and have children. Another reason is for a husband and wife to show love to each other through the unity of making love.

A third reason God designed sex for people is because it feels good. When a husband and wife make love, it gives them both an extremely pleasant physical sensation—an orgasm, or climax. An orgasm gives a person an all-over warm, floaty, tingly feeling that lasts for just a few seconds to a minute or so. After this feeling passes, the person feels relaxed, content, and happy.

Sexual intercourse leaves you feeling very close to the person with whom you've made love. That's why it can only be shared by two people who are married. Do you know what the word *vulnerable* means? It means you have let someone see who you are in your most unguarded state. Making love with your husband allows both of you to be vulnerable with each other and still know that your emotions and body are safe with each other. For some couples the experience is so intense and satisfying that they cry when they make love.

Physically speaking, a woman cannot get any closer to her husband than to have a part of him literally inside of her.

Another interesting point about sexual intercourse between human beings is that people are one of the few mammals that make love face to face. Have you ever seen animals mating? The male usually climbs up on the back of the female to insert his erect penis into her vagina. But God designed humans to experience the pleasure of intercourse face to face. He created it this way for increased feelings of closeness and intimacy.

MASTURBATION

The word *masturbation*, also called self-stimulation, means rubbing parts of your own body to give yourself an orgasm. When a husband and wife make love, the part of a woman's body called the *clitoris*, a little knob of flesh located right above her urethra, is rubbed while her husband is sliding his penis in and out of her vagina. This is what creates the good feelings she experiences during intercourse. Maybe you have located this spot for yourself when you have been touching yourself or washing. It feels good to touch it. Perhaps you have found that when you rub that spot, you get pleasurable feelings.

There are many varying opinions about whether a young man or a young woman should masturbate. It won't harm you physically. But God did create those pleasurable sexual feelings to take place inside the context of marriage. At the same time we do not believe you need to have feelings of guilt if you do explore your body. Our feeling is that this is a personal choice you need to discuss with God. Dr. James Dobson in his book *Preparing for Adolescence* says, "It is my *opinion* that masturbation is not much of an issue with God. It's a normal part of adolescence that involves no one else. It does not cause disease, it does not produce babies, and Jesus did not mention it in the Bible. I'm not telling you to masturbate, and I hope you don't feel a need for it. But if you do, it is my opinion that you should not struggle with guilt over it." Our hope, along with Dr. Dobson, is that you will want to and be able to wait to experience those pleasurable feelings until you are married.

MAKING LOVE . . . ANYTHING LESS IS JUST SEX

All this talk about sexual intercourse may make you uncomfortable with the thought: *My parents do this?* Yes, that's how *you* got here. Some married couples make love several times a week; others make love only a couple of times a month. To your parents, making love is a normal part of their lives together. It's like driving a car or showering—only a lot more enjoyable!

The feelings of closeness that sexual intercourse produces must take place between two people who are married and committed to loving each other no matter what. Making love can only occur inside the safe place of a marriage.

Let us give you an example of what we mean. Imagine giving a treasured piece of jewelry to your best friend. How would you feel if she lost it, gave it away, threw it in the trash, or just didn't value it. You'd likely be hurt, angry, and disappointed. You may not even be able to look her in the face again. Most of all you'd be mad at yourself for trusting her in the first place with something you treasured.

That situation is similar to your virginity. You are a virgin until you have sexual intercourse. God has given you the gift of your sexuality and virginity. If you take this gift and give it away without much thought, you will never get it back. If you have sex before you are married, you've given away a treasure God entrusted to you—your virginity and purity. If you choose to have sex before you are married, the young man with whom you've shared your purity might not take care of the treasure of your sexuality. He may use it and then likely cast it away—not taking into consideration your feelings. And you can never get it back.

YOU CAN NEVER REGAIN YOUR PURITY.

ONCE IT'S GONE, IT'S GONE!

Virginity is the ultimate gift you can give to your husband, and him to you. You can only give it away once. It's the perfect wedding present: Your entire sexual being. On your wedding night you can tell your husband, "Here, I've been saving myself just for you, just for this day." Isn't your purity worth saving for the man God has picked out to be your husband?

STILL A LONG WAY OFF

We know this all may seem as if it's so far in the future that you don't need to think about it. But if you make a decision right now, *this very minute*, to save your virginity for your husband, you won't need to think about it again until you're considering marrying a man. Up until then there will be no need to consider making love with a man. You will have already made the choice not to, *today*, this minute.

Even go so far as to write out a promise to yourself in the space below. Write the promise in your own words or in these words: "Dear Lord, I want to keep myself pure for the man You will have me marry someday. I promise to stay a virgin until my wedding night because I want to give my husband the gift of my body as a wedding gift. Lord, help me to remember and keep this promise."

Now sign and date what you've written.

Good for you! We're proud of you!

Keeping Your Body, Mind, and Soul Safe

What is one of the most important things you've learned so far from this book?

YOU ARE IN CHARGE OF YOUR BODY!

We've explained how God designed your body, how your body functions, what to expect in the coming months and years, how to stay healthy, and a little bit about your future with the man God has chosen to be your husband.

Now we want to talk with you about ways to be sure you stay safe. Because you are in charge of your body, there are things you need to do to protect yourself.

NO SHARING

We know this may be the opposite of what your parents have taught you in regard to your brothers or sisters. Let us explain what we mean when we say, "Don't share."

We all have germs in our bodies. Those germs actually work to protect us from other harmful germs. But some people have germs, bacterial or viral, in their bodies that aren't good. These can cause various illnesses, and some of the illnesses can be very serious.

These dangerous germs can be spread to you through
contact with someone infected with them. The problem is
that the people with the germs may not look or feel sick. So
you don't know whether they have the germs or not! The
type of germs we're talking about aren't like the ones that
cause colds or stomach flu. The dangerous germs cause serious life-threatening diseases such as AIDS or hepatitis.

Just casual contact with people who have these diseases
will not harm you. You can talk with them, play games with
them, sit next to them, and play sports with them. You *cannot* catch either AIDS or hepatitis by being friends with someone who is infected. The Bible even tells us to be friendly to
others who are ill. They need to know you care for them.

BUT . . .

You should never share items with them that have
touched their *mucous membranes* or their blood. Mucous
membranes are any entrances into your body—mouth, nose,
eyes, vagina, and anus. What sort of things do we mean?

NEVER SHARE A SODA CAN, ANY DRINKING GLASS
(EXCEPT AFTER WASHING IT), TOOTHBRUSH, RAZOR,
NOSE TISSUE, UNDERWEAR, SWIMSUIT, WET TOWEL,
OR EYE MAKEUP.

It is a good, healthy standard to live by to avoid sharing
these things with anyone—even your best friend! Just make
it a rule for your life. It will help keep you healthy and protect you from diseases.

SAY NO LOUDLY

We think it's probably likely that your parents have discussed with you things to do to stay safe when you are alone
at home or away from home. Now is the time to review

those guidelines with them. Remember that the guidelines and rules are to protect you!

Even though you are likely safe almost all of the time, there may be times when you find yourself in a situation that makes you feel uncomfortable. It's sad to say, but we can't trust everyone around us. There are people who are fascinated with young women and, if given the opportunity, could hurt you. We aren't trying to scare you. We just want to help you to *think* and *act* in ways to protect yourself.

SARA

Something really scary happened to me last year. I was at the mall. (Of course! It's where I spend half my life!) I was waiting to meet my friend Rachel at the bookstore, but she was late—as usual. I wandered around window-shopping, not really paying attention, when all of a sudden I could feel someone looking at me. I moved to another window, and I could see the reflection of a man standing behind me. My skin felt really prickly. Knowing he was watching me made me very uncomfortable. I walked toward the bookstore, and I could see in the store-window reflections that he was following me. Then I got really, really scared! I half-jogged, half-ran to the bookstore and picked up some book about architecture next to the checkout. Right—like I'm really interested in buildings, but I knew I'd be safe near the counter. I saw the guy walk slowly by the store. I pretended not to notice, but he looked right in at me. Then he just walked past. I was still feeling shaky by the time Rachel showed up. The rest of the afternoon I felt jumpy, and I kept looking behind me wherever Rachel and I went, but I didn't see him again.

I told Mom what happened. She got kind of upset, but she told me I did the right thing by sticking close to a checkout counter. Then she went over all those "safety rules" again.

Sara showed "smarts"! She immediately found a "safe place" where she could tell someone if she needed help. It would not have been safe for her to make eye contact with the person or confront him by talking to him.

Why was the man following Sara? Who knows? Maybe he was just trying to scare her; maybe he wanted to ask her something; maybe he was thinking about kidnapping her. But Sara sensed danger, and she thought and acted in a safe and responsible way. Discuss with your parents these and other ways you can stay safe:

☞ *Trust your instincts. If you suddenly feel scared, you probably are in a threatening situation.*

☞ *Always tell your parents exactly where you will be, who you will be with, what you will be doing, and how long you will be away from home.*

☞ *Always go places in groups of two or more. Agree on a place to meet in case you get separated.*

☞ *Never confront, talk to, or provoke in any way someone who is threatening you.*

☞ *Never get into a car with someone without asking your parents' specific permission first.*

☞ *Never accept food, a drink, candy, or an article of clothing from anyone outside your usual group of friends and family.*

☞ *Never agree to have your photograph taken without talking to your parents first about who is taking the photos and why.*

☞ *Remember, even someone you think you know could be a threat to your safety.*

If someone is persistent in bothering you or you feel threatened:

☞ *Put up a big fuss!*

☞ *Say "NO!" repeatedly and loudly.*

☞ *Be rude. Don't have a conversation with anyone you don't know.*

✍ *Call 911 and tell the person on the other end of the line where you are and what is happening to you.*

✍ *Call on the name of JESUS. Loudly and repeatedly say, "IN THE NAME OF JESUS, STOP!"*

We need to ask you to promise us and yourself something. If *anyone* speaks to you or acts toward you in a manner you find threatening or that makes you feel uncomfortable, please tell your parents, a church leader, or your school counselor. In order for them to help keep you safe and make sure other young women are kept safe, they must know about any situations you have seen or been a part of. Will you promise us you'll tell?

SEXUAL HARASSMENT

Sometimes people may go even further than just doing or saying something that makes you uncomfortable. This is called *harassment*. If anyone touches you, talks about your body, makes sexual comments, or repeatedly asks you for dates when you've said no, that person is sexually harassing you. This is not only wrong, but it's against the law too! There are laws to protect you from people who want to make you feel uncomfortable about your sexuality.

Again, it is so important for you to tell an adult you trust when someone is sexually harassing you. The adult can help you work out a plan to stop the harassment. Don't try to take care of it by yourself. Get help!

SEXUAL ABUSE

Sexual abuse is when anyone—man, woman, or someone your own age—touches you in a sexual way. This means touching, brushing up against you, pinching, kissing, inserting anything in your rectum or vagina, or any other type of caressing that is meant to make you feel sexual. Because you've made a commitment to stay pure until you're married, it is never okay for someone to try to "turn you on" or force you to have sexual feelings.

We realize this can be a very difficult situation if it is happening to you. First we want you to know: *It is not your fault.* Even if you have participated in this kind of relationship, and it has felt good, it is still not your fault. The person doing this to you is not healthy in mind and needs help. You may even have strong feelings for the person touching you in a sexual way, but you must stop the relationship.

We also recognize that you're scared if this is happening to you. You likely know this person well; it may even be a family member. The person may have told you that bad things will happen if you give away the "secret." You know things will change and may get very difficult when you tell, *BUT YOU MUST TELL!*

The first thing to do is pray for help to remove yourself from the situation. Jesus wants to see you in a healthy relationship. He wants to help you. He is also the Great Physician. He wants to heal you of this unhealthy relationship.

We bet you already know the answer here. That's right— find a trusted counselor, church leader, or parent and tell the person *exactly* what's happening. The adult will get you the help you need and will support you during the coming days.

We cannot stress enough or urge you more strongly to seek help *today* if someone is sexually abusing you. You have the right, the ability, and the strength to stop it now!

PORNOGRAPHY

Pornography is photographs, TV pictures, movies, or online computer images of naked men or women and/or men and women doing sexual things. Looking at pornography is a very dangerous habit to get into, and that's just the thing—it is habit-forming.

The pictures are meant to stir sexual feelings in the person viewing them. Remember your commitment to stay pure until you are married? Pornography may not result in an actual sexual act for you, but it does put sexual thoughts and images into your mind. Are these pleasing to God? We don't think so. Pornography spoils the purity of your mind.

God meant sexual intercourse to be a very private act between a married couple. Showing naked people or people having sex in a magazine, on TV, or on-line on a computer is not very private, is it? These images take away the beauty and privacy that God intended. The pictures aren't a true example of God's plan for a pure sexual relationship between a husband and wife.

Have you ever felt a little funny about seeing a kissing scene on TV or in a movie? Maybe you felt embarrassed or shy about watching. God put those feelings there. The reason you feel that way is because your inner spirit knows that kissing and other sexual acts should be private—not shared by an audience. We don't mean to say you shouldn't watch programs or movies with light kissing. That's fine if it's okay with your parents, but we think that any more than light kissing isn't okay and may give you the wrong impression of what a godly married sexual relationship is like. The best way to avoid getting involved in viewing pornography is not to start in the first place.

ILLEGAL DRUGS

We're sure you've heard this message at school, but it's always worth repeating. *Say no to drugs!!* Let's talk about why.

Plain and simple—drugs kill brain cells. You need all your brain cells in top working order to accomplish all the things you want to do with your life. Remember your list from chapter 6 of what you like to do and want to learn to do? If you take drugs, you might hurt your brain cells so much that you couldn't accomplish those things. Would that be worth the few short minutes of feeling good from drugs? No way!

Why do people take drugs? To feel good. Drugs can give people a "high." They make the users feel as if everything is going great. But you know what drugs really do besides kill brain cells? They make you lose control of your body for a time. Drugs change the way you think. They can confuse you and therefore get you into a situation where you aren't safe. Knowing that you want to stay in charge of your body means that you definitely don't want to use drugs—not even once!

You might wonder exactly what we mean by drugs. Drugs can take the form of pills, alcoholic drinks, cigarettes, other substances to smoke, powders that can be inhaled through the nose, and liquid substances in syringes and needles to inject into the body. If anyone offers you anything like one of these, say no and walk away. Even if a friend offers you something, don't accept it. And think about that. Would a true "friend" want you to do something to yourself that is going to hurt you? We don't think so, and we bet you don't either.

EATING DISORDERS

A person with anorexia or bulimia either does not eat enough to nourish the body or eats and then makes herself throw up before the food is digested. Binge eating is related to these—a person eats a huge quantity and then makes herself vomit. People with eating disorders also frequently use laxatives to make themselves go to the bathroom a lot. Some also have a very strict exercise program that may include hours every day of working out.

An eating disorder happens when young women (and sometimes men) don't feel good about the way their bodies look. They may think they are too fat or not attractive in certain areas of their bodies. Eating disorders start because the person has a warped sense of how the body should look.

We again are going to challenge you to be truthful here and now. How do you feel about your body? Have you ever thought about or indeed changed your eating habits because you have felt that your body is too fat or not perfect enough? If you have answered yes, please hear what we have to say:

YOU ARE PERFECT JUST AS GOD CREATED YOU!

Now we want you to go back to chapter 5 and reread what we wrote about God's design of your body. Then come back to these pages.

Why are eating disorders so dangerous? The scary truth is that you can die from an eating disorder. If a person does not eat enough or intentionally vomits what is eaten, her body starts to break down her muscles and bones for energy. Her heart begins to beat erratically—sometimes enough to cause a heart attack. She stops having her period and eventually will damage her internal female organs so much that she'll never be able to have children—all just to be thin. Is it worth it?

We can answer: *No, it is not!* Both of us authors know personally women who have suffered from this disease. This isn't one of those diseases you can catch. It starts in your mind. And we want you to know that there are ways to prevent it from happening to you.

First, if you are unhappy about how your body looks, talk to your mom or another Christian woman whom you trust. Tell her exactly what you are feeling. Tell her you are afraid you could develop an eating disorder. If you already have started experimenting with your weight and limiting your food, tell her that too. Pray for the Lord to help you see yourself in His eyes. Pray that He will help to take away your fear of being overweight or out of control of your eating. Every time you start to think obsessively about your weight or food, think about the WWJD saying. Indeed, what would Jesus do?

This is another one of those times when you need to make a commitment to yourself to stay healthy. Be firm with yourself, talk to yourself, and force yourself to eat. With help from caring adults and really believing what God says about your developing body, you can learn to like how you look right now and how you will look in the future. No fair comparing yourself to how others look. This is about *you* and God's perfect plan for *you*. Though you may not like the way you look now, remember you are "becoming." God's not done with you yet!

We can't express enough just how important it is to trust your parents and church leaders with questions and concerns you may have about what is going on in your life, particularly the things we discussed in this chapter. This has been a difficult chapter to write and probably a hard one for you to read. But we know you need to be told the truth about things—including some that are unpleasant and scary. We know you are intelligent, and if you are faced with any of the situations we talked about, you'll do the right thing.

And remember what we said at the beginning of this chapter: You are in charge of your body! H-U-G yourself and feel proud of all the good choices you've made so far and the excellent choices you'll make in the future. We know we're proud of all the positive commitments you've made to yourself in this chapter for your physical, emotional, and spiritual health and well-being!

Now we'd like to talk about other plans God has for you during your continued path through puberty and for your life in the future. Is God working in your life right now to prepare you for the future? We can answer *absolutely yes!* As you read this last chapter about God's plans for your life, pray that He will show you, give you some insight, about the person He wants you to become.

God Has a Plan for You

We wish we could meet every one of you in person. Why? Because you each have such wonderful potential. We know that without even seeing you! We know you each have gifts, skills, and interests that God has entrusted to you, and it is so exciting to think of the possibilities for your life! That's why we wish we could talk with each one of you, to watch you embrace and get excited about what's happening in your life.

YOUR FUTURE HOPE

Your life is like a huge Christmas box. This present is wrapped in bright multicolored paper with a thick fancy ribbon wound around its middle. A shiny bow on the top completes the intriguing package. You don't know exactly what's inside, but you're pretty sure you'll like it because the One who gave it to you knows what you enjoy. The box is so big it takes a long time to open it, almost as long as the time it takes you to grow into a young woman. Once the paper is removed, guess what's in the box? All the gifts and talents God has given to you! They are like new clothes, each one waiting for you to try on and use. There will be times you'll use one more than another, but they are all there, the special gifts He has given you for you and for His glory.

What exactly are the gifts in your box? We can't answer that for you, but we do know your gifts are the interests, talents, and spiritual ideals He has given you. Do you have a strong desire to tell everyone about God? Maybe you have the gifts and skills to be a missionary. Do you have a deep compassion for people who are hurt or animals that are suffering? Maybe God has given you the gifts to become a medical worker. Do you like to teach children and friends about things? Maybe God's plan for you includes child care or teaching.

Proverbs 23:18 says, "There is surely a future hope for you, and your hope will not be cut off." What is your "future hope"? Go ahead and dream! If you could be anything, do anything, what would it be? Sail around the world? Be the mother of ten children? Be a missionary in South America? Be a politician? Build houses? Own a farm? Run an orphanage? Be a doctor? Maybe you have a variety of interests and can't choose one over the other. That's fine! The more interests the better; it will be fascinating to see how God will bring them all together.

You certainly don't want to plan your entire life right now, nor should you. But what you can do is start thinking about certain skills that you can learn or develop in your areas of interest. Let us explain. We'll use Lori as an example.

LORI

I love nature, being outside, walking, listening to the birds, looking for animal tracks on the side of the road. Animals and how they live and think is really interesting. Do squirrels just "know" where all the yummy nuts are, or do they tell each other somehow? Maybe that's why I want to learn to ride a horse, because I just want to be part of an animal. I want to understand how it thinks.

I love animals, just about any kind, except maybe scary ones like alligators. I like to read about them and dream about having a bunch of my own someday. My mom says maybe I could be a veterinarian when I get older. The problem is, I don't like school very much, and I know you have to get really good grades to be a vet.

Even though a decision about what Lori wants to be as an adult, and more importantly what God wants her to be, is very far off, she can start researching or looking into different areas that interest her.

Because her interests revolve around animals, she could start by volunteering at an animal shelter. She would likely clean cages, feed animals, and perhaps help with some medical procedures. This would give her an opportunity to see if she truly liked working with animals. She would want to pray for more opportunities to look into working with animals. She might progress to working at a horse farm, again cleaning stalls, feeding, and general care. Eventually, if animals still captured her interest, she might be able to get a summer job at a local vet's office, zoo, wildlife preserve, pet store, or farm.

What has Lori gained from all of this "work?" Several things. First, she has gathered information to decide if this is something she wants to work at as an adult. Second, she has learned the responsibility of doing a job. And last, she has gained self-confidence in her abilities and skills. What if through all this she learns she can't stand being around sick animals? That's terrific! She has lost nothing, only gained a deeper understanding of herself and crossed off a potential career. She hasn't wasted anything by backing off from this possibility. Because:

NO EXPERIENCE IS EVER WASTED!

You learn a lot about yourself when you have different experiences. And you can put what you've learned to use in the next interest you pursue. Sometimes God may give you an area of interest just for a short time, and maybe His long-term plan for you will be different from what you think it might be now. Either way He will equip you and give you the desire to do what He wants you to do.

YOUR LIFE PLAN

Don't get scared away by the term "life plan." As we said before, we don't think you should plan out your entire life now. What you can do is explore your various areas of interest to gain knowledge and skills for a potential career.

Like Lori did, you can think about doing jobs that would give you more understanding of your interests. These "jobs" may be volunteering, observing, or researching.

Start by considering what profession you might be interested in pursuing. Then break down that profession into different categories that you could learn more about. For example, say you were interested in being a doctor. Name all the aspects of medicine you can think of, such as private practice, surgeon, research physician, pediatrician, etc. Break these down even more into the one or two areas that interest you.

Say you want to be a pediatrician. This kind of doctor cares for sick children. You now have two major questions about this profession. Do you like kids, and how do you feel about sick kids? Maybe you don't know the answer to either question. That's fine, but the way you can find out is to try working with children.

How can you start caring for children? A good place to get practice and instruction is in your church nursery. Your church probably has policies about when, how, where, and with whom you can help in the nursery, but ask your pastor or youth leader to help you get started. It also is a good idea to take a "baby-sitter certification course" through your local hospital or family resource center. Once you have this qualification, then you can baby-sit for families and gain more experience—one step closer to determining if this is something you want to pursue further.

Making a life plan is like playing with building blocks. The base or foundation is your general interest in one area. You build on that base through various experiences, adding more blocks with each "job." You can plan which blocks you need to add to build upward to reach your final goal.

We'll give you another example. Let's say you want to be a writer. Right now at your age, you can start writing whatever you want to. That's your foundation. You can find out more about the profession by visiting a newspaper office. You've added a second layer. Next you could do an extra-credit essay paper for your school and ask your teacher for special help in writing. You could also help produce a school newspaper and write articles for it. You've added a third layer. When you reach high school, you could take college preparation courses in journalism, English, and literature. You've added a fourth layer. You could start working for a local newspaper or magazine writing for their student page. You've added a fifth layer. Do you see how each previous experience builds on the last one and brings you closer to your final goal of being a permanent writer?

But what if after all those years, you're sick of writing and decide to do something entirely different? Fine! As we said before, you've wasted nothing and gained insight into yourself. The great thing about building your own life plan is that it's *yours!* Change it however, whenever you want! Many people end up doing something different from what they studied in college or what they thought they wanted to do when they were teenagers.

The point of a life plan now, during your younger years, isn't to decide on a long-term profession. It is to give you a purpose, something to focus on during your teen years. It gives you something you can feel good about, something that will increase your self-confidence. It helps you to stay focused on goals during the years when so many other influences compete for your attention. Making and building a life plan will ultimately protect you from many of the challenges that teenagers encounter everyday—peer pressure, drugs, or hanging around with people who have lower spiritual standards than yourself. When you have a life plan in mind, you can look at the other influences and decide if they will add another layer to your life plan or take a layer away.

GOD'S PLAN

Jeremiah 29:11 says, "'For I know the plans I have for you,' declares the Lord, 'plans to prosper you and not to harm you, plans to give you hope and a future.'" He does have a specific plan for you. His plan does include the interests, skills, and gifts He's given you.

God's plan for you is like a big picture book, huge, opened up in His lap. He has your life all planned out; it's already written in this book. Each colorful picture shows you at different stages in your life. He knows and *sees* what will be happening in your life. Right this minute, as well as when you're an older teenager, a young adult, a mature adult, and an elderly person. *He knows it all now!*

A well-known writer, Tony Evans, says that God in heaven sees your life as a long parade. You are walking in this parade, a part of the action, but you are limited and can only see what is directly in front of you and remember what you have passed behind you. You can't see around the next corner or over the next hill. But God can because He is up above looking down, and He can see the whole lineup in front of you. He knows what's around the next corner and over the next hill. Your responsibility to Him is just to stay in line and trust Him to guide you on the right route.

As the verse from Jeremiah says, God's plan is not to harm you, but to prosper you. That doesn't necessarily mean your wallet. He wants you to flourish, to grow in mind, body, and spirit. His plan for you is exclusively yours. His plan was written in His big picture book before you were even born. He knows you so well, better than your best friend, your mom or your dad, that His plan is *perfect for you!*

Remember, we said at the beginning of this book that you are on a journey? Do you feel more prepared now to face the road ahead, the parade ahead? We've given you the tools you need to continue to march and grow into a woman—mind, body, and soul. As you undergo these changes, keep your eyes focused on what God wants you to be. The transformation God has set in motion in your body is one of His challenges that will help you grow up. The changes you see and feel happening in your body aren't what God is doing to you; they are what He is doing *for* you, to fulfill His plan for you to be a godly young woman.

APPENDIX A

ॐ

If you accepted Jesus Christ as your Savior as a result of reading this book, write a note to the publisher of *Just for Girls*, telling them about this life-changing decision. They will send you more information on how to live as a Christian. Send your request for information to:

> Jutti West
> Good News Publishers
> 1300 Crescent Street
> Wheaton, IL 60187

Do you have questions or comments for the authors? We'd love to hear from you. You can write to us at:

> E. M. Hoekstra & M. B. Cutaiar
> Direct Path Ministries
> P.O. Box 103
> Dublin, NH 03444

BOOKS YOU MIGHT ENJOY

Dobson, James. *Preparing for Adolescence*. Regal Books, 1989.

Miller, Donna. *Growing Little Women: Capturing Teachable Moments with Your Daughter*. Moody Press, 1997.

The One Year Bible for Kids. Tyndale House Publishers, Inc., 1997.

The One Year Book of Devotions for Kids. Tyndale House Publishers, Inc., 1993.

Hostetler, Robert, ed. *Josh McDowell's One Year Book of Youth Devotions*. Tyndale House Publishers, Inc., 1997.